The Art of Sanity
Creativity Complexity Sanity

By David Courtney

Also by David Courtney:

Theory of Mind (2016)

The Art of Sanity
Creativity Complexity Sanity

ISBN: 978-0-9951521-2-0

Contact David at d.courtney@bell.net

Thank YOU

Thanks to Dr. George Seim for perusing my manuscript and offering comments. Most of all, I'm thankful for his enthusiasm, for his being willing not be dismayed by unintelligibility. Knowing that someone is paying close attention to your writing is the best possible encouragement. When George commented 'beautiful writing' it fueled my efforts again and again.

Thank you, to my wife Christina, who for many moons now, has been my rock of Gibraltar. Whether driving in the very challenging city of Zurich Switzerland or working her vast array projects she is, and always will be, the love of my life. We're still like two kids exploring this thing called life. Her huge painstaking effort on my manuscript is more than appreciated. I get near the finish line and she carries me across.

Also a big thanks to Bill Hancock of Media House: always very human, and very creative, and for a little producer like me, an absolute God-send.

Table of Contents

The Art of Sanity

Poetry – the Lenny Poems

Screen – a dramatic play in two acts

INTRODUCTION

CREATIVITY AND SANITY

The Art of Sanity is awkwardly written, I must confess. For that I apologise. However, the point transcends the writing. Just reading the quotations will feed your mind, your soul, and your psychological balance. This is a difficult thought experiment. I hope it is just my immaturity as a writer challenging sight in a world willfully blind. If, in places, you despise my tone, I'm with you on that one.

Like Archimedes, a bath will do it for me, or hanging on the inversion board. A bike ride or walk in nature will also get the juices flowing. I've always thought there is a psychokinetic aspect to creativity. Each of our cells assumes the posture of polarity. By patterning our reality we establish metabolic conditioning and fall prey to entrainment.

How we choose to step outside the conditions of entrainment is what art Is about. Beyond the developed and too frequently acknowledged patterning of our daily bread circuitry, our cells are oxygen deprived. The generative forces need balance and fluidity. Without fluidity, the synaptic juices ferment causing entanglement issues.

This is modern man's most prominent feature: an attention span not up to snuff in developmental strategies involved in the continuum of consciousness over a lifetime.

I see reading the introduction of this book as a litmus test for dementia vulnerability. If you can't muster the attention span to haul in the understanding the intro offers, your attention span continuum is dis-eased.

Creativity is liberty from the sort of daily patterning that refutes the soul. Creativity refreshes the screen. The fountainhead of reality is triggered as we escape the foregone conclusions in our lives.

The influx of patterning in modern humans breeds frequency entrainment throughout the self, in terms of polarities and hence postures. These postures immerse us in crystallizing features that cause brain atrophy. The brain's retreating electrical system can short-circuit and cause innumerable breaches in the system. These contaminated circuits manifest as various mental illnesses, all causing types of dissociative features in the brain. In Bi-polarity, Depression, PTSD, the mind is lost to predispositions and hence at a loss for what to do. Most approaches are to push the person back on the tracks, eternally repressing the psychology of urgency. This makes people cranked to perpetual, superimposed fight and flight.

In more extreme mental illness, taming and stabilizing urgency is like breaking a horse. You make the condition suitable for riding. Oftentimes, this regulates the psychokinetic potential in an ever-subjugated fashion, patterning the true self out of existence. The ability to plasticize becomes a challenge. Neurogenesis, the birth of new neurons becomes a highly compromised activity. Spontaneous joy is trapped in so many contrivances it doesn't ever happen. 'Now' becomes a fable about some future possibility.

Creativity is a psychological release that activates cell polarity as a groundswell of self-interest motivation. It doesn't work well under the threat of expectation. Expectation puts its back against the wall, where, once- measured, it is sure to come up short. Deep is the prejudice in mental structures constantly manifest in our most intimate self.

Following The Art of Sanity, you'll find some of my creativity: poetry and a dramatic play. There is a poem on depression written a decade after being depressed. It is a rear view mirror re-allocation and re-affirmation. There are some of my Lenny poems, dedicated to my life-time (through listening) partner in crime, Leonard Cohen. I never get sick of plumbing the depths of Leonard. And yes, Leonard had some shallow parts as well, which makes him human. He's the guy overtaken on the roof and the guy who brings your groceries in. He's also the guy who knows how to get used to a lonely room.

SCREEN - THE DRAMA

This play, in part, is about an organization named SET, which stands for Subjectivity Enhancement Teachings.

Lance Ericson is submitting himself, without reserve, into their workshops which means mind formatting exercises.

His girlfriend, Scarlet Éclair, sees him losing his grip on reality. She sees him falling into their clutches.

The play involves a big video screen and much of what goes on is interactive with the screen. This is where SET's workshop material unfolds....the screen exerts an hypnotic element.

Across the back is the big screen and a cupboard and couch.

The dynamic involves Scarlet constantly phoning as Lance is mentally preparing himself for his baptism into the metaphorical élite at SET. She's worried. What he sees as growth, she sees as indoctrination; what he sees as self-exploration, she sees as Jonestown massacre. Scarlet's phone calls contest with the SET stuff on the screen. In the second act, an alien arrives as a Jungian transplant projection, materializing for the first time in centuries as the impersonating presence of Iota.

"Happily for me I have not found my style. I should be bored if I had," Dégas.

PREFACE

I'M A LUMBERJACK AND I'M OKAY

In the early grades of school we were shown a black and white 16 mm film on the logging industry. Big trees were hauled to the river where they would join an armada of trees floating downstream. A most unfortunate occurrence was a log jam. A jam would be profoundly difficult to address as layers of huge trees would necessitate a shutdown of operations. Imagine pick-up sticks in a complicated pile. It would take a lot of man-hours and heavy lifting to get things back to normal.

We are currently in a log jam of information. It happens innocently enough with the Media chasing down ratings. Dr. Phil and Dr. Oz have to take more and more scandalous approaches. Like with opiates, the dose has to go up for the same effects. Pretty soon there is a lot of drama going around, just treading water with ratings.

There are log jams in the mind. What was once clear was once the truth is no longer obvious. Information is stacked on information. The confusion poisons balance in the brain. We become willing to see only one side of the issue.

There are none as blind as those who refuse to see.

Brains are fired and wired into place. Sometimes they are bent out of shape by experience and firing and wiring takes off in a wrong direction. To manage a hundred billion neurons with trillions of activities is difficult. As M. Scott Peck says in the opening of his book, The Road Less Traveled, life is difficult. Life is an experiment in time. Things can go wrong.

And to top it off, there is real time fastened to finite chronology and there is mental time, a little more fluid.

PATHOLOGICAL LIAR

When a person mentions pathology it is usually in the instance of pathological liar. A pathological liar just can't help themselves. They lie, for whatever reason, as a matter of course.

This we would describe as a necessary way of doing business because of some quirkiness in the psyche. They can't change their spots. However conditioned into being, within the domain of its origins, it now exists as a psychological fact.

People learn how to lie so they can sidestep the truth. When syndrome takes over a person, it is the overtaking of the psyche by automaticity. Eventually the things on automatic pilot have the vote, the popular support in the realm of selfdom. Automaticity is like clearance credentials. Automaticity means low degree of scrutiny. Chronic or Pathological liars start early. It is a developed behaviour. There is what is called a fabricated tendency that precludes much behaviour orientation. Interestingly, such liars do exhibit stress and guilt when monitored with lie detection equipment. Psychopaths have zero conscience detectable when so monitored. Lying and telling the truth are the same to a psychopath.

During the frantic and cowardly response to the Communist threat during the McCarthy years, America was said to exhibit Security Syndrome. This means a certain pathology takes over the population. The mental pathways on amber alert are directed through the checkpoints of concern. Concern makes for greater caution on subway platforms, in popular markets or at airports. Fear can log jam a population.

There are other pathologies like Nationalism and Patriotism.

People can always be stoked when it comes to Patriotism even though they don't know their neighbours from Adam. If Alien invaders suddenly appeared, coming in our direction, we would be united as Earthlings on the planet and our patriotism would take on a sudden global dimension. We can't see that because of the log jam of national interests that aren't national interests, simply business interests.

Pathology is dangerous; most so because it restricts the mind outright from developing in certain ways.

When one is thinking about their security, they pro-actively engage syndrome thought-processes. They become more nervous, more cautious. This is why Big Brother in 1984 juggles the spin, keeping everyone on edge, their lives forever tentative. Eventually everything is syndrome-matic. The status of thoughts becomes organized and prioritized. Growing up in the majority of households individuals run a high risk of mental inbreeding. Guided by entrenched automaticity it is hardly any wonder octogenarians get lost taking a simple walk around the block. The notion of 'lostness' predates our arrival. Getting lost walking around the block is, I believe, connected to simplest expedience methodology in the brain. We over time simply forget to take a look around. Our motivation and our pathology put the nose firmly against the grindstone and the grind is on. After going into the convection currents of modulating brain modalities, it is a startling thing to raise your head and take it all in. The scenery has been erased incrementally. This block you have found yourself on is new to you; you've never seen it before. Indeed, the block you remember is attached to a subdivision you lived in twenty years before.

The constraints we put on our minds by assuming a rigid disposition creates a pathological awareness with an entire range of derivative values as to what this means. What it dictates is scope and scale. It's a cage with a controlled vista...a view through a window in the psyche carrying out designated biases including entrenched fear. You never get to be yourself and so you forget yourself over a life time. Forgetting the trees and the grass is part of it.

The biggest problem with Sanity in a syndromatic society is the closeness to the edge between existence and non-existence. When History comes knocking, the cushions are off the couch and the couch blocks the door, and people are shouting GET DOWN. Many people are already there. The pathology of Fight/Flight is superimposed in every moment. We are anxious.

Most of everything comes down to a person's me-you-it relationships. You have a complex brain. You didn't ask for it. In many ways it is more complex than you are and you fail to acknowledge its complexity as a matter of course.

Most people round off fight or flight to the nearest round number. We deal with it. We can't not deal with it. It gets under our skin and ratchets the ante up in the brain.

Swimming with the current takes all our energy. Swimming against the current is unimaginable. Being swept along in the mainstream leaves little room for self-realization and truth.

BEHIND THE GREEN DOOR

Behind the door on the left is PERPLEXITY. Behind the door on the right is SIMPLICITY.

It's up to you.

Which one?

Or put it this way...behind the left door is the book of riddles and tales of history and behind the door on the right, a case of beer. People like to keep it simple. We are at the point of the general landscape of mental hyperspace that keeps a person lockstep with over bite. When you are pathologically bent out of shape you miss the chance at self-realization by a country mile.

When we communicate we transfer information. There are various ways of depicting the information transfer. A story is a memorable thing hence highly desirable. An event, like Newton's apple may not have happened but speaks volumes as to understanding. It sums it up. Conveyance is guaranteed if the story is a good one. It's hardly surprising that myths and religions use stories to inform us of crucial narratives. Apocryphal is the label given to stories that may or may not have happened but regardless continue to happen as stories, and continue to inform we humans.

Such a case involves Sir Isaac Newton: his famous moment when the apple fell on him triggering an a-ha moment that history considers duly remarkable and justifiably so, the discovery of gravity. (It might have been the same apple that took down Steve Jobs and Alan Turing.) Indeed, the apple has played significant roles since the Garden of Eden, most famously with Apple records and Apple Computers

HOW DO YOU TELL A STRANGER 'BOUT ROCK AND ROLL?

Let's say it's a couple thousand years ago and someone explains the meaning of levitation by which he means elevating the self above the daily grind. How do you depict this if, by this, you mean the levitation above worldly desires, hence a mental perspective? It would be easy to confuse a mental depiction with a depiction of a physical event.

For the scientific mind things became podal and antipodal in the moment-to-moment functional domain. Bigger, smaller, farther, closer - dark and light help us think, help us stratify and structure thought. This is where causality, if-then- therefore happens. Compare, contrast, schematize happen here. It's also where logistics can set up apparatus and prove something hypothesized extending thought into action and back to thought.

Einstein did nothing with a Bunsen burner, or microscope - nothing until he met Hubble, with a telescope even. Einstein's apparatus was his imagination. His thought experiments are well documented. The mind constructs an intangible reality made out of thoughts growing into other thoughts. The document of thought is a document of intangibles.

'Listen to the Rhythm of the Falling Rain' is a song by the Cascades. It starts with a burst of thunder and appealed to the film maker in me. It depicts a guy listening to the rain which tells him over and over that he's been a fool.

> LISTEN TO THE RHYTHM OF THE FALLING RAIN
> TELLING ME JUST WHAT A FOOL I'VE BEEN

This notion of self-reflectiveness bouncing out into the world and coming back as 'RAIN' and as atmosphere is a simple rendering of communication beyond linearity. In other words, a symbol or metaphor can enrich communication exponentially.

Despite the obviousness of this as communication, little is done to teach the human mind how to teleport the imagination through thoughtful pictures. It's so obvious in a song like this, and it forms the basis of most Art.

When I'm talking about formatting the mind I'm talking about altered states of consciousness. There are all sorts of altered states. Pilots flying high and divers going into depths often experience altered states. Drugs induce altered states. Being nervous is an altered state. Anything different from your normal everyday consciousness is a differentiated or altered state.

THEY ARE COMING TO TAKE ME AWAY

If you've allowed yourself to be entangled in the day-to-day without the big picture compass, your very sanity for the long term is at risk. Your normal way of doing business organizes your mind in a way that compromises the integrity of the whole, over time.

People no longer have their wits about them. Everyday people are falling into dementia, because they don't recognize the street they are on from any other street. Their mind structures have forfeited the ability to cohere.

If these people were having their minds stolen by Aliens it would be front page news. Ours is the great befuddlement. When we stare mental illness in the eyes of loved ones we flinch. We are at a loss to strike a course of action.

The day of reckoning is always, unavoidably now, in neural networks. Their polarization is in place, shaped by growing up, and over time, much too much is outsourced to automaticity. This results in MIND-SET.

Mindset is a peculiar beast. As a teacher I was all too familiar with the sort of kid who walks in the classroom door saying, I'm going to fail this test. One's perceptions of self can, of course, evolve. This kid can come around, but often theory becomes fact and the kid programs himself for failure.

This isn't the only sort of mindset though. A friend in high school had a horrible alcoholic father from whom he was estranged. His brother was a high achiever, very successful, very bent on putting his father's identity and his as far apart as possible. His mindset prevented him from smelling the roses. Many consumed by full-throttle ambition have the trigger event in childhood. It becomes their most devout need. Often they don't balance their life experiences. Their capacity for emotions has had short shrift at the hands of the ambition.

Eventually my friend's brother succumbed to Parkinson's. I mention him because of a documentary on TV on PTSD about reporter Curt Petrovich who visited some gruesome and terrifying events as a reporter. From this exposure he developed PTSD. Curt's father in the segment appears gruff and condescending.

Here is my analysis. Curt has never measured up for his father; he actually says this.

The only story Curt works on during his rehab is the story of Robert Dziekanski, a Polish man visiting his mother in Canada. His gruesome Taser death can still be viewed on YouTube. The cops, for no good reason, had murdered this poor man.

The police in the Taser airport death are power figures just like Curt's dad.

His PTSD, he feels as weakness, a weakness his father has always spotted in him. This weakness is something inside him that exists because his father instilled it in him.

His father and the police, by demeanour, are of a similar cut. The reason Curt sides with the police is because he sides with the father against his own self. The reason I mention this case is because of its complexity and, paradoxically, its simplicity. Curt assumes he is at fault for not measuring up to his father. He never blames his father for being a jerk. He blames himself.

This twists Curt's mind into a brain loop distinguishing features erroneously and attributing erroneously. It's simple Freudian transference. By supporting the police he is finally standing up and identifying himself with them. He is a man.

His audacity in approaching the Polish man's mother is symptomatic of mind blindness. He hasn't put himself in her shoes. More importantly he never put himself in the Polish man's shoes arriving at a foreign airport unable to speak the language, treated like an animal.

Though he identifies with this Polish man in the sense of being a victim, he has no empathy for him or his mother. Mind blindness is built on a foundation. These are bricks and timber as you structure yourself and find yourself most at home with constituent firing and wirings.

These firing and wirings determine experience agenda and hence capacitation proclivities. We often can't see what is in front of our eyes. Here is a woman who lost her son to unfeeling, arrogant power- tripping police. Sure the police got unfairly treated in the perjury trial, but that was sidebar.

The kid who thinks he's going to fail an English test might retreat to a job where reading and writing plays a small part. We retreat from the ways of unknowing to the ways of knowing. The incumbent self moves forward, give or take a little shrapnel.

Unlike cars and planes, you steer your life without a visible instrument panel. There is no air traffic controller.

Think of it. A hundred billion neurons on the gallop and nobody at the helm to marshal reality in a self-optimizing fashion. The guy who thinks he is at the helm is simply a piece of architecture reflecting mindset. That mindset can easily unwittingly bring a person down because it artificializes and depersonalizes.

ANOTHER HURT KURT

It's hardly a stretch to connect the dots in Kurt Cobain's life from his parent's divorce and his scrawling on the walls to his Teen Spirit to his suicide. The way our brains get around to taking us down is becoming neuroscientifically evident. They are many.

Mindset is clearly a result of a need to have a mind structure. To have a hundred billion neuron universe without structure would be scary. Freud and Jung and Reich covered a lot of psychoanalytic territory. The consequences from rigidity to psychosis are incrementally taking over because the information juggernaut has too much information and too little heart.

We are complex structures, but given the current state of the information-bombarded brain we are hijacking ourselves constantly. To stand on the riverbank and witness the flow of life is important. I've tried to get people to read things that would help modify their mind structure for the better but they are attracted to the stream of entertainment slash sports, completely plugged in to an idea of self reflected back from what they are plugged into. They can't step aside that flow of information to gather the self.

At any rate, I see many males who have constructed an idea of self from which they won't budge. They will put a fence around that character and stock guns on the shelf to protect it. The strictures of this one-on one superimposition are antithetical to firing and wiring anything other than confirming redundancy loops. The incumbent self wins hands down.

The need to defend the mind comes from an insecurity--a thought that trying life in a different pair of shoes might be more than can be handled. This is the fundament dilemma for modern day psychology and for every person on the planet. Who or what do you follow? Is there a golden way or any way at all?

Most of course worship, though they don't call it worship, the contemporaneous world. If everyone is, as the Bible suggests, on the broad road that leads to destruction, then our nemesis might be surprisingly near. We've fallen in love with technology and just when it seems a match made in heaven it all goes wrong. Minds once coherent start babbling incoherently. Anything can go wrong when our instrument control panel is buried in psychological motifs testimonial to the highly charged reality childhood creates. The problem seemingly occurring simultaneously is this coming to terms with the reasons for one's mental architecture being the way it is--unbending even in the face of deep need.

When I was depressed it was like torching my past life. Burning bridges became first and foremost. Like Samson I was pulling the whole world down on me. I did it my way and the consequence was an all pervasive drowsiness that captivated my molecular existence. I was a dead man walking at the bottom of a dying ocean.

Is there an Absolute star to steer by?

The knight of faith on the quest of life could make a leap of faith over the abyss and live in a transcendent state uncompromised by the daily manifestations of a pre-occupied trivial-pursuits culture. This ability to relativize mortal coil finite reality with a knowledge based on faith was behind Kierkegaard's idea of an absolute connection to the absolute. The absolute, first and foremost, is a connection based on extraction from the entanglement features of Group Think. It is not absolute in the sense of being tangible and place-able in the firmament. It is a condition of the heart. It involves empathy and conceptual evolution of life-script. Based on your library of symbols and imagery, your intuition and your sense of self-growth, your moments of breakthrough

An absolute connection to the absolute is like antennae picking up a signal in space, a signal known by its pulse not its location. It fits right in with Heisenberg's quantum uncertainty principle, Godel's incompleteness theorems and Wittgenstein's 'measure' of mathematics. Reality is a force and it exhibits this form, as frequency, a frequency being a pattern.

The pattern for humans can best be visualized as a guinea pig experiment. Imagine the guinea pig is blitzed by flashing lights and big screen, little screen optical engagements, and more flashing lights and noise, burning a hole in your frequency range.

Eventually the poor guinea pig can't think straight and starts banging its head against the cage.

In human terms, absolute is a conviction that evolves. It is the self-revelatory trajectory that delivers one from the harassment of bombardment.

Chapter 1 - UNDER THE UMBRELLA

I live in Canada. Sometimes our winters are fierce. Freezing snow can cover you in a flash. Getting stranded in a snowstorm can be deadly. Freezing to death is a reality risk.

Winter clothes, hoods and parkas insulate us, keeping warmth in and the cold out. Insulation in your house works similarly. It is a blanket. It protects your environment from the elements.

Insulation can look much different, of course. When we look at wires, say speaker wires, we peel back the insulating plastic to clear the wire to hook up the speakers. Similarly electrical wires of different gauge present varying thicknesses of insulation.

We have a similar coating of insulation in the brain. We have insulation active in our brains so our electricity doesn't cross circuits and explode in a fireball of tangled wires. In the brain, insulation is called myelin. It coats axons, preventing them from deviating into other circuitry. Insulation insulates what is from what isn't. Our loyalty to certain habits establishes thicker coating and more expedient routes.

Speed limits are gauged by how we stylize our brains. These are myelin enforced in respect of density. Your user-friendly, go-to circuits are densely inaugurated. They fortify and protect our personality against damaging blows.

To create our minds, we fire and wire. Many think of the synapse gap like Evil Knievel jumping Snake Canyon. It's really more like two motorcycles catapulted from ramps on each side of the canyon. Potentiation happens on both sides of the gap.

The environment is ripe for certain types of potentiation and not for others because of the firing and wiring that patterns itself into the brain. Potentiation is a meaningful state in the brain, assuring more attachment to brain plasticity and the fountainhead of new neurology. This is called neurogenesis, which consists of the birth of brand new, baby neurons.

The contrivance of living, and what it takes to get by in the daily grind, automatically positions us in firing and wiring habits. We become insulated according to physical and mental constraints the give and take of being physical, and being social and conscious all in one go. Our firing and wiring takes on the look of a familiar self. Our neural map has been shaped by our desires and constraints in innumerable ways. Literally, we are talking a hundred billion neurons, with trillions of connections. Our neural maps are victims of culture, of vocabulary, or range of ideas mitigated through the self-construction process. This sets up polarities, as the way we feel and think about things imprints us into view point and vantage point. Before we know it, we are entangled. If the way we are entangled refutes being psychologized for mental health, we become mentally unhealthy. Particularly, we ring up attention span deficit when we need a functional continuum of mindful attention span to keep the ship afloat.

Calvin, a third generation neurobiologist, has established coherent understanding of the neuron's vector alignment. Each neuron develops a weighting; a leaning into its disposition for firing and wiring. These weightings are directly related to personal narrative. Things imprint from our narrative. Not a big surprise that personal happiness or tragedy imprints big time, vectoring up the gravity of our responses. It's nice to have the science to know the psyche's interrelatedness in measurable ways. Big feelings create major weightings in our neurons.

If our neurology vectors point to pre-emptive stylization of reality, we become close-minded.

The signal to noise ratio in the firing and wiring loses ground when velocity of information exceeds the relativizing factors. What is comfortable for one stage of our lives may become uncomfortable later on.

If intelligence was somehow identical with brute force, then barbarism would be inevitable. As we evolved, we realized, for mutual benefit, we must cut others some slack. You don't want to fight at every drop of the hat. This civilization was fashioned on ideas about freedom. It evolved so we wouldn't be governed by knee jerk responses. Our world and its invasiveness has produced much mental illness.

With the brave new world of technology, this generation of ideas has eclipsed the past with frightening regularity. We no longer stand on the shoulders of giants. We are a society made barbarian after hundreds of years of development because we are defaulting on our commitment.

The digital world has no historical counterpart in the minds of children. They know no difference. They become fired and wired in the oven of mass media.

They are oblivious to what really matters, and simultaneously, unsurprisingly, hounded by mental illness. Shallow minds are not up for the complexity the human brain demands. Constrained to short term memory and frontal cortex spin-a-thons, the human brain plays havoc with mindfulness.

Evolution was smart. It realized arrogance is a defence mechanism employed by the insecure. Annihilators annihilate each other. The Meek therefore will inherit the Earth. Often, only the beaten, drowning man sees the need for salvation and change. Weakness as strength is built in. **There is a crack in everything, that's how the light gets in**...as Leonard Cohen sang, and it's true. Like Paul on the way to Damascus in the Bible story of his conversion, sometimes getting knocked on your ass makes for epiphany.

William Blake cautioned us more than 200 years ago about pulling children from the echoing green, lining them up two by two, and sitting them down to categorical bookending. The imagination is something that needs to find its own depth. Taking the child's mind and tying it up with schooling prematurely dismisses so much growth out of the starting gate. Recently, school boards have instated accounting classes in elementary school. This is a complete outrage to the developing imaginations, including feeling and thought structures. We are an autistic culture, and we do it to ourselves by hurrying kids into being adults living between the red and the black.

COMING UP FOR AIR

This book is a direct response to my upbringing and most people's upbringing. The lenses we looked through to see the world were put in place when the world was different. They don't fit the circumstances anymore. And it's bloody difficult to adjust.

Like a ball of wool you start pulling at, surveillance simply reveals more and more strings attached to more and more muddled knots. Most often there develops a cleavage in the very notion of reconciling past and future into present. There are many who believe stirring things up leads to trouble, adds insult to injury.

The subconscious is ignored and a gadget drive full of the latest apps becomes the surrogate mind. The surrogate mind scuttles here and there. It gets by. Getting by is the name of the game.

When pressured, the present doesn't exist. Present, or at least a present that you have true presence in, is harder and harder to find. Your life goes by in a blur. You hardly get your foot in the door of tomorrow, forget about today.

ORANIZING THE JUNGIAN PERSONA

There was a movie out entitled, A Beautiful Mind, which implies, what many think: it's pretty much convention to think, that Mathematics personifies the precision of a beautiful mind. Stated another way, to think like a calculator is efficiency personified. The pieces fit. The puzzle adds up.

Though we know mathematics from our school days of readin' writin' and 'rithmetic we know little about the men who developed it and flushed out its far-reaching diametric and applicability.

Three of the mathematical giants right up there with the name of PYTHAGORAS, are Godel, Wittgenstein and Whitehead. Godel came up with a mathematical proof about the impossibility of completeness within a mathematical system. In other words, following the reality of mathematics, one is led to an incompleteness theorem, in essence an abyss where logistics and numbers don't add up, where mathematics can't prove itself.

Mathematics is necessarily incomplete. It's not absolute or infinite. Within its walls are wormholes. Wittgenstein agreed in a sense his monumental work Tractatus.

Tractatus 6:52 espouses there are indeed things that cannot be put into words. They make themselves manifest beyond the means of words to convey. They are what is mystical. Language, of course, manifests itself with descriptiveness of what is the case. Whether it be a truck or a butterfly, you can admit it into consciousness, you can bank it, know it. Mysticism, when you try to download it, or import it, or Wikipedia it (thank God for Wiki leaks) is representational. You cannot connect the dots on mystical. It is a manifest word and the fact a man who stood completely peerless (having shed Bertrand Russel) said this, is a profound thing said. Wittgenstein travelled to the edge of mathematics, not through philosophy but through mathematics.

Human interaction by a mathematically explicit human mind would simplify existence one would think.

This is very much not the case. Like Autistic Savants, high functioning Mathematics types often have a proclivity very much out of step with others. Their reality is too often a tortured one. Godel weighed only 65 pounds at death. Most know the anguish suffered by Alan Turing after the war. Before the Enigma-solver became the historical Turing his life was hell on Earth. Wittgenstein had the benefits of a Savant while simultaneously being existentially and artistically challenged by his circle. Gustav Klimit painted Wittgenstein's sister. Famous composers frequently visited and one brother was a touring concert pianist. Three of Wittgenstein's brothers suicided established benchmarks for Ludwig's existence.

A beautiful mind, if by that we mean a mathematically organized mind, is not a mind that adds up to social ease. Quite the opposite.

To think of the mind in terms of machinery is becoming a clearly deficient concept. Neuroscience at long last is revealing the overarching role of subconscious and unconscious realms. To speculate that the perfect life is a life that runs like clockwork is a gross simplification of what is truly up.

BEEP BEEP

The entire genre of thinking that erroneously sees in mathematics the desirable nature of the human mind is well settled into the mainstream

Ways of seeing ourselves have been reduced because of a loss of a bigger language: the language of Art and Analogy and Metaphor and Vision: that can dance circles around arithmetic.

Math plods on the dance floor. Math is conceptually axiomatic to itself. That we can grid reality against its methods is pure superimposition. Axiomatic math is good at illustrating things that it can address. On everything else it has zero jurisdictions.

The fact is something it took me a lifetime to realize; everyone is vested in who they are: from the Mathematician to the Saint. This seems obvious, as to not be invested in who you are, would put you at fundamental cross-purposes within the self. What is not so obvious is the manner in which we arrange ourselves accordingly, to prevent cross-purpose conflict.

This is entirely dangerous in respect of mental stability to be at cross-purpose unless one is intentionally reversing field to liberate the self. People's cliques and groups promote vested interest realities. Someone from outside can cause deep consternation if and when values are challenged. Indeed dissociation springs from minds at cross purposes and blossoms into mental illness.

Plastika from the Greek characterizes plastic as something poured into a mould. The human mind is that malleable, that it changes itself. It's NEUROSCIENCE and old neuroscience at that. You pour your patterns of firing and wiring into a mould, a self-concept parlayed with the world, designed by circumstance, endorsed or refuted by experience. This is the demographic as statistical biography, the present, an elusive document at best.

In the formatting of the human mind you need to anchor reinforcement steel and anchor bolts. These come through digestion of experience and how that experience shapes psychological and physical patterning, implicating underpinnings as it goes. How you structure your firing and wirings is your responsibility. In a world too much with us there needs to be push-back if one is to have enough elbow room to understand freedom.

UPPER CRUST

Many people see Art like the art in the Louvre...stately, regal scenes capturing the pages of history, the likes of Napoleon on horseback or Marat in the bath tub. They are great but two hours of walking around the Louvre will grind you down, bring you to your knees. This is stately art.

Not so the more flamboyant arts that challenge your vested interest self. The gallery in Zurich, Switzerland, enlivens the mind at every turn. Same with the Musée d'Orsay and, for the most part, Le Pompidou. Art keeps the mind alive. When vested interest becomes complacency and complacency becomes automaticity we need art to pull our souls from the abyss.

KEYSTONE COPS

My mother used to look after the Police Answering Service. The Police were one of her customers on the Orangeville Answering Service back when people had dial phones and no way of leaving a message.

We never got any call for the police. The police force of 4 or 5 had no problem 'controlling' a town of 4000. The biggest threat was a bar room brawl turned ugly. Other than that it was a sleepy town.

Now the town is bigger and the police force exponentially so, is way out of proportion, which begs the question: are we evolving, are we becoming more civilized or less?

In a movie, Jean Luc Goddard says, 'images are murdering the present.' implying the screening of stuff through our mind is like a wheel of fortune, a wheel that never stops spinning. Where do we fit in to this new world, if fitting in is trending away from our security?

JUST ANOTHER JOSEPH LOOKING FOR A MANGER

Leonard Cohen sings, 'he's just another Joseph looking for a manger.' How does an ordinary guy deal with life when there is no room in the inn?

Our endless chase inside the self, replicates itself in endless patterns, patterns difficult to rein in...often more a part of us than arm or leg. Who are we outside the circumstantial evidence of driver's licence and voting history?

A few months ago another women's story got less than decent coverage. A bus was travelling through Nigeria....on board were Christian women and Muslim women. The bus was stopped in the middle of the desert by a host of gunmen. They told the Muslim women to step aside, get off the bus. They wanted to shoot the Christian women. Instead, the Muslim women sprawled their bodies over the Christian women telling the men to shoot them all. Faced with this show of courage, the gunmen left.

The mind is so much more malleable than we ever imagined. So much of it is incidental accidental. The Shape of self, of inherent beliefs and attitudes is likewise malleable. Evolving one's own morality is a steady course of knowability. We live in a time that reveals not so much Barbarians at the gate as behind the desk, the pulpit and the lectern.

Things are coming to a head. What goes on in Guantanamo Bay is a much accelerated and invasive version of contemporaneous society. God help us, for what we humans do to each other in the betrayal of where humanity could have gone.

"Guantanamo Bay is an experiment in brain washing...when first detained, prisoners are put into intense sensory deprivation, with hoods, blackout goggles and heavy headphones to block out all sounds. They are left in isolation cells for months, taken out only to have their senses bombarded with barking dogs, strobe lights and endless taped loops of babies crying, music blaring and cats meowing...resulting in ...

...this inmate 'was evidencing behaviour consistent with extreme psychological trauma (talking to non-existent people, reporting hearing voices, crouching in a cell covered with a sheet

for hours on end)...." (Mamdouh Habib in The Shock Doctrine by Naomi Klein, p. 51).

GREAT EXPECTATIONS

"The synaptic architecture of the cerebral cortex defines the limits of intellectual capacity, and the formation of appropriate synapses is the ultimate step in establishing these functional limits," (John T. Brewer, Neural Connections: Some You Use Some You Lose).

This book is about the formation of appropriate synapses. The trajectory of appropriation of territory is such that the mind always goes to the focal point of most attention-span gathering event to the next. Without a strategy for the formation of functionality it follows the path of least resistance.

Functional limits are a concept that is ultimately more meaningful than other things because it is first and foremost in determining the mechanisms by which we discern what is first and foremost. What is definitely a first for the human brain is the need to sort out information on the run. The formation of appropriate synapses is the firing and wiring that comes into play as one conducts the business of being. What seems

38

appropriate in the formation is virtually inbred into us. Beyond that, society at large shapes us with expectations and expects us to be normal. We haven't gotten collectively to a point of no return. To find that one's firing and wiring is not an aspect of physical declension is foremost. Placebo dismisses once and for all the myth that physicality is the only thing on board. Indeed we have been too enamoured of mickey mouse mentality that can recognize causality in only in its most meagre form, located almost entirely in the tangible world. It is everywhere in our understanding. Blake called this the mind-forged manacles. The initiative that our mind takes is produced by our broader circuitry including mainstream manifest culture.

"Pruning is influenced by environmental factors and is widely thought to represent learning. After adolescence, the volume of the synaptic connections decreases again due to synaptic pruning. Some neurons and connections are killed off. With pruning there is a retraction of neurons that are not functionally appropriate," (accessed Apr. 19, 2017, Wikipedia – Neuron Pruning).

Functional appropriation ends up succumbing to what is called Automaticity. The human approaches automaton status the more a creature of habit he or she becomes. Unfortunately, the feelings quotient takes a beating in this regulatory habitual environment. Feelings are not programmable, or if they are, they become affectation or role playing. As one ages, activation of motivation is directly relational to brain plasticity which in turn enervates via Empathy and the emotions.

What seems functionally appropriate is the nature of self-engendered by one's narrative habits, including more than anything an uncensored by rationalization of the ups and downs on holding a self-sustaining course. Self-sustaining means being employed or married or whatever and this eclipses the primordial conviction that at its core originated and defined what being sustained means.

It turns out Man does not live by bread alone. Can't. Won't.

He lives by psychology a psychology often pre-empted by Pathology.

These are not categorical things but felt things. Your cognitive world boils down into feelings or lack thereof. The difficulty arises in this very realm as habit erodes feeling. Feelings become faked or contrived in some way shape or form creating a lack of ambience. The number of neurons coming on board (580 000 per minute in a baby) is countered by a massive pruning involving billions of neurons. You are shedding neurology as fast as you get it which demonstrates the ferocity of interface.

The emphasis on any individual's life story or narrative is key to self-hood. Neurons have weighted vector descriptiveness demonstrating polarity and establishing boundary regions in appropriateness. Pretty soon you can't fire and wire your self out of the framework which presupposes a definition of destiny within its own constrained logic a socialized version of destiny in linear and chronological terms. To say pruning is influenced by environmental factors is understatement. The left brain has an agenda of cause and effect trapped in scope and scale. The strategy of weightings, influencing the vector and speed the narrative back and forth, altering the synergy of the system. The energy outside the box is attainable through non-appropriated thought.

Within a closed system energy runs downhill. Eventually there is not enough energy to reach the further out areas of the brain. Motivational lapses establishing lower electricity thresholds rule the day. The brain suffocates itself as unused-ness in the brain overwhelms the cognitive structures. Reciprocal action is built into the brain by neuroplasticity and neurogenesis at scale of complexity within the give and take.

Creativity can reciprocate and hence resuscitate because it gets something from nothing, something tangible from an intangible means. Sustenance rests solely within the realm of the well-orchestrated brain and the well-represented self. With narrative vector being profoundly important in polarity and capacity we must nurture sustenance not refute it. Creativity is the very nature of neurogenesis, and to a large extent, neuroplasticity.

Chapter 2 – <u>ALL THE WORLD'S A STAGE</u>

I am an old man, a dull head among windy spaces….(TS Eliot)

> "Man, proud man, drest in a little brief authority – most ignorant
> Of what he's most assured,
> His glassy essence – like an angry ape,
> plays such fantastic tricks before high heaven
> As makes the angels weep," (Shakespeare)

The singular, most daunting problem facing us is a misappropriation of values. As TS Eliot says here, most ignorant of what he's most assured is the characterizing reality everywhere apparent.

Where we go, who we are, is becoming a question of some proportion. It all seemed so obvious a couple decades back. Society was a well-oiled machine. It needed tweaking of course; issues of justice must necessarily evolve. We were on our way to getting it right.

So much for that narrative. We have refugees and terrorists, not to mention all-pervasive lack of trust in politicians and the entire political system. Security brokered down to he who hacks best.

PLAYING WITH THE UNIVERSE

Nobel Prize-winning Richard Feynman was chuckling to himself. Indeed, the more he thought about it the more outrageously ridiculous and funny it became. He was getting offers from universities across the country including, perhaps the most ridiculous, the Institute for Advanced Studies where Einstein was. Einstein's bosses wanted him. Hilarious. It's true he had had a good run with his Master's project and degree but now he felt burnt out. He was wasting a lot of time hanging out at cafés watching the girls go by. When that got boring he'd head home and read Arabian Nights. At the same time as he was assailed by doubts he was enjoying his teaching position. Wherever he was at, physics, he found somehow disgusting. It wasn't fun anymore.

"So I got this new attitude. Now that I am burned out and I'll never accomplish anything, I've got this nice position at the university teaching classes that I rather enjoy.....And then I thought to myself, 'you know, what they think of you is so fantastic, it's impossible to live up to it. You have no responsibility to live up to it!'....I have no responsibility to be like they expect me to be. It's their mistake; not my failing...

THEN A FORTUITOUS EVENT IN THE CAFETERIA: A SPINNING PLATE

......It was effortless. It was easy to play with these things. It was like uncorking a bottle: everything flowed out effortlessly. I almost tried to resist it! There was no importance to what I was doing, but ultimately there was. The diagrams and the whole business that I got the Nobel Prize for came from that piddling around with the wobbling plate," (Richard Feynman in Creators on Creating, p. 67).

Today, a school in Toronto is banning cellphones from in-school use. This is crucial. Cellphones dish out connection and instant gratification, looping the mind continuously through a series of shallow poses leading nowhere. The smokescreen for technology is everywhere. What is up with education is simple: an ever increasing attention deficit, making for an inability to continue a thought and add it to more thoughts over a continuum. Attention deficit is bound to grow as we become more and more wired to less and less that is substantive. The result is ignorance: an inability to possess continuous development.

When one steps away from this attention-deficit ingratiation one realizes how little growth has occurred in the human mind. We have, for one thing, barely inkling about how survival could be managed if technology fails. There are necessary strategies in mindfulness if we are not to fall victim to putting all our eggs in one 3D printer basket. The average graduate knows next to nothing about growing crops or raising animals or having enough vision to see how things are kept in their respective priority. Technology, like the unsinkable Titanic, is such a glow worm and the world basks in its light.

FEED YOUR HEAD

Starvation of the mind is a little more difficult to address. What features of essence that fundamentally enhance evolution are crucial for mental health continuance? How do we get out of this looping, this forgetting of self, one moment to the next? Mind constitution feeds on the thoughts we feed our heads. If we don't do our mental push-ups we won't be able to do the heavy lifting required for big ideas. There will be no option but to be herded like animals towards an unapprehendable future.

Why do we need big ideas? Our brains are complex. One hundred billion neurons are not happy with a brain that cuts itself short. You prepare a place to live in your mind by firing and wiring it into place. Its orientation, including capacity orientation, is part of the firing and wiring, the scale and scope.

Innerness, continuum - whatever we call it - is disappearing like it never existed. Innerness is becoming more and more definitively contradistinctive to the ongoing superficial engagement of the everydayness of the everyday world. **The world is too much with us, its coming and goings, said Wordsworth, 200+ years ago.**

'Its coming and goings' in the early 1800's when Wordsworth lived was much slower than our coming and goings today. The contagious speed of coming and going is undermining any measured response we might have.

I am the messenger, I am not the message. The fact is the world is coming at us faster and faster. The message is: we fail to heed what's happening in our heads to our peril. That is the important thing here. I'm saying that all mental illness is pathological. It's not air pollution or water pollution that is the cause of mental breakdown. The fault, dear Brutus, is not in the stars, it's in ourselves. Mental breakdown happens because of the corrosive nature of the building materials, in terms of psychology and emotions. We outsource our psychology. The minds we are building these days aren't up for the long haul.

OUT OF MY TREE

All I've done is draw together insights and research already out there. Each neuroscientist is located on his branch of study, comfortable in her or his work environment, entrenched within a specificity zone of highly co-ordinated reality checks and balances. That imprisons them in their area of specialty. Absolutely none of the neuroscientists have the time to spare given the super-structure of the science community and the funding criteria. Who is there to synthesize and configure a big picture of neuroscience? Now, more than ever, it is a picture anyone can connect the dots on with a little scrutiny in respect of a handful of overarching considerations. That's what this book is about: those overarching considerations.

Autism is a spectrum. Depression, bi-polarity, dementia are all spectrum conditions. Symptoms are less or more and that's what spectrum means. There is a range. All this involves superimposing a scale of severity of symptoms. Like a gas tank, it can be closer to empty or closer to full. The spectrum demarcates levels of behaviour and controllability and defines treatment approach parameters.

Everything is spectral.

THE COURTNEY SPECTRUM

My spectrum, I'll call for usage purposes, the Courtney Spectrum. What it measures is inter-subjectivity in tandem with empathy. These I will characterize throughout the book as more complex exercises in humanness. In its simplest recognition, an Autistic child will not have enough inter-subjectivity to recognize nuance in a conversation. At the left end (imagine a protractor with 180 degrees) of the spectrum are Male Extremism, Psychopathology, Asperger's and Autism. What these all have in common is damaged inter-subjectivity and less capacity for empathy. In the case of male extremism this is a desirable trait in their valuation. Upholding maleness means toning down empathy and inherent within empathy is conceptual awareness. The male brain looks at life through a lens that is all or mostly ego.

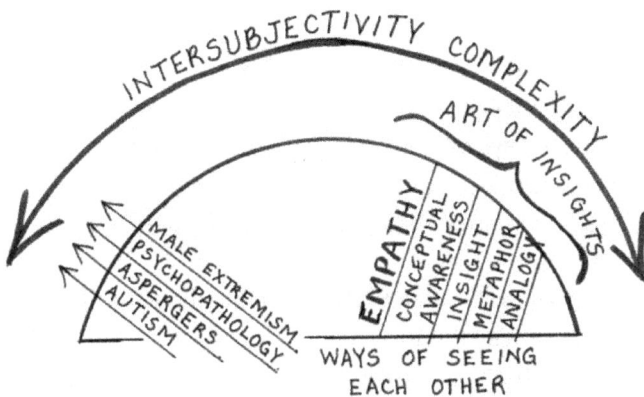

INTERSUBJECTIVITY COMPLEXITY

ART OF INSIGHTS

MALE EXTREMISM
PSYCHOPATHOLOGY
ASPERGERS
AUTISM

EMPATHY
CONCEPTUAL
AWARENESS
INSIGHT
METAPHOR
ANALOGY

WAYS OF SEEING
EACH OTHER

Essentially, the Courtney Spectrum is an inter-subjectivity spectrum. Intersubjectivity is also identical with conceptual complexity. Inter-subjectivity should not be confused with being social. It is more an inter-penetrating chunkology at work. The more you move from zero inter-subjectivity, the more subjectivity you acquire, the more mirror neurons per cubic inch. Things are conveyed like thought shapes as we read other people. Mirror neurology is structural and embodies more of other people, the more empathy and insight we have. A person with high inter-subjectivity will use that discernment to distance social-interaction that compromises the self. He does this by looking at the big picture mythology; the archetypes at work against the measure of one's own benchmarks.

Autism is, of course as mentioned, a spectrum unto itself. In its most extreme state it is short on inter-subjectivity, and theory of mind and mirror neurons. Chunking hunks of others into a self-appreciation by synthesizing events doesn't happen for them. Nuance, in terms of tone or body language, doesn't happen.

Inter-subjectivity is manifest most richly in art, literature and ideas, not to mention psychiatry and philosophy. Here there are non-logistical ways of 'chunking' experience, which is an embrace to the extent of EMBODIMENT, including metaphor, analogy, etc. A fountainhead of everything creative is here.

For me as a painter and poet, the analogy of mirror neurons works just fine. Call it mirror neurons or not, the configured association of brain areas points to conceptual imaginative activation. VISION is MIRROR PLACTICITY IN MOTION.

"Perhaps because of such doubts, many of those working in social neuroscience chose not to base their arguments on mirror neurons, but on the limited claim that the social brain consists of brain areas specifically attuned to the recognition of different aspects of conspecifics – individuals of the same species – such as faces, motion, and attribution of mental states, some of which seem present at birth, and others of which develop over time. As Sarah-Jayne Blakemore puts it: the social brain is defined as the complex network of areas that enable us to recognise others and evaluate their mental states (intentions, desires

and beliefs), feelings, enduring dispositions and actions, [Blakemore, 2008, 267]," (Nikolas Rose and Joelle M. Abi-Rached, Neuro; the New Brain Sciences and the Management of the Mind, p. 147).

In other words, whether we agree with mirror neurons or not the truth about specially attuned evaluation areas is proven. In the complex nature of self, there is nothing more complex than inter-subjectivity.

"Few would doubt that there are neurobiological conditions for our capacities to impute feelings, thoughts, and intentions to others, or for our capacities to engage in social interaction," (Nikolas Rose and Joelle M. Abi-Rached, Neuro; the New Brain Sciences and the Management of the Mind, p. 147).

The message is succinct. The neurobiological conditions for just such capacities exist. There is no argument to suggest otherwise.

Activities engage mirroring and cause proliferation of more mirroring, more depth to the mirroring.

Something in the coining of the term the Courtney Spectrum can symbolize so much. Think of how the term THEORY OF MIND has now been utilized to explain so much. By using the Courtney Spectrum we can symbolize inter-subjectivity status.

IMMUNE TO THE MOON

By walking a mile in someone's shoes you can alter your perspective. This includes a complex arrangement of connectedness. In its most astute form it transfers sensibility as in art.

This is profound when it comes to self-understanding. The more you mirror the other person's experience from their thoughts to their emotions to their environment, the more you grow in conceptual amplitude. You know more about yourself by knowing more about them.

What we have to address is this inner need to strike out of existence our inter-subjective pursuit because of conflicting energies within the self. This is why people are in a mood for racism and hate crimes because of diminished (log jammed) subjectivity, a defensive subjectivity becoming normalized.

It is becoming more universal to simplify and objectify who we are.

"It was by way of theory of mind we are able to attribute mental states to other people, in particular to attribute beliefs and false beliefs to them [Adolphs, 2003, 171]," (Nikolas Rose and Joelle M. Abi-Rached, Neuro; the New Brain

Sciences and the Management of the Mind, p. 144).

To be discerning at reading people, seeing how attached to their beliefs they are is a most significant exercise for the human brain. To read another's motive package not only reveals the potential of a problem but the potential of a cure. It shows why NBA star Kevin Durant, a pensive and thoughtful guy, is more aligned with a Steph Curry than a Russel Westerbrook, the latter being (at this stage) more a physical guy than a mental guy. It's why LeBron is functionally different from a Charles Barkley or a Shaq.

In sports, where competition is hinged to physicality, the pensive guy is the exception.

The Aquarium Principle: the size and complexity of the brains of primates, including humans, are related to the size and complexity of their characteristic social groups. (Nikolas Rose and Joelle M. Abi-Rached, Neuro; the New Brain Sciences and the Management of the Mind, p. 143).

You wouldn't expect a professional athlete to veer far off the prototype. The promise of mirroring is no less dramatic than depicted with Jason of Golden Fleece fame and Medusa. By holding a mirror to slay Medusa, Jason has modified reality by reflecting it in a perspective that is utilizable. That's what we need to do. Corporate psychopaths or leaders like Donald

Trump could gain mirroring ability. The outcome would be a pleasant one. Imagine.

Imagine a discussion of G20 leaders during a yoga laughter class.

We can, all of us, move on the Courtney Spectrum. Insight and creativity are one and the same. Such creativity emerges from knowing how to hook up one's narrative to the ethereal womb where anything can be born.

"What if it was the case that our sociability, like that of our primate ancestors, was a consequence of the evolved capacities of our brains, if our group formation was shaped by our neurobiology, if our empathy was not merely social but neural? And what if our neurobiology does not just establish the conditions for sociability but also the forms that it takes? What if our friendships and our loves, our communal ties and hates, our social and cultural lives take the shape that they do as only a consequence of our neuronal architecture? (Nikolas Rose and Joelle M. Abi-Rached, Neuro; the New Brain Sciences and the Management of the Mind, p. 142).

This is precisely my point. Neuronal architecture is brain formatting

The z-particle between the photon and a boson is just such an intermediary hybrid. Like Schrodinger's cat, it's never the case that a point in time can determine its state, as in the case of the cat, whether it is dead or alive. This in-between-ness is precisely the modulated reality of a creative action. In human evolution this is precisely what goes on. And once evolution started betting on the mind, and consciousness, as the NEW APPENDAGE, everything changed. Hence forward, evolution has banked on the mind. Going down the list, unquestionably consciousness was the game changer. For sure, the evolution of the mind held more promise than developing physical attributes.

The Mind is where we could organize nature so we wouldn't have to be hunters and gatherers whose survival is subject to the lottery of good and bad fortune. After all, it was with the mind we were able to trade-in the cave for the condo.

But the mind is a curious thing. As Freud, Jung, Reich and others pointed out, the mind has a way of becoming scattered and eventually turning on itself.

I have come to the point blank assessment that all mental illness comes from a lack of emotional capacity and resource to deal with stress.

Our spirits rebel. We feel a deep-seated need to come off as more than the mortal coil finitude statistics embalm us with. It's the nature of these very conflicting energies that imprint us and put us somewhere on the mental health spectrum. Manic and depressive trajectories are there. To the manner in which we subsume our identity we owe our mental health or mental illness. No one has perfect mental health. We all have our ups and downs. Some downs become ruts. Some ruts become graves.

You might want to shoot the messenger, because as messenger I may end up doing you irreparable harm, in deconstructing your idea of who you are. Your idea of who you are is too much with you for you to know who you really are. We need to separate you from your surrogate identity. We'll need to take a look at your image-making machinery and the servers, serving up your downloads.

The thing is this: plasticity becomes all-too-often irrevocably established. It becomes your neural map. The map you are at ease with is a map in a map, a technological labyrinthine reality no man has ever confronted ever before in human history. It is a map dis-eased with information. A map as a result of media implemented boundaries. Who you are not is less and less part of the picture. Every day you fire and wire who you are. That's great; it lets you sleep at night to be an identity recognized as you. It lets you get mail with your name on it. This identity, it turns out, may, however, cease to be the right thing for you going forward into the passages of middle age and aging beyond.

Being anchored to an increasingly dysfunctional self is no picnic. Yet this is becoming the new narrative.

That, in fact, is the necessary realization here: your responsibility to your life time in the plasticity continuum. The plasticity taking shape now is the plasticity you live in tomorrow. You are a marked man or woman. A specimen equal to all random specimens and your peculiar reality might actually prove the catalyst for a step forward.

You cannot shirk duty here. No one on the planet is as responsible as you are for your brain. You are unique. We're all in the same boat. I'm on the hook with everyone else.

What we are on the hook to is our plasticity.

Of course plasticity has a backdrop. Genetic forces exist in your family tree.

LOVE AT FIRST SIGHT

Given my relationships I can't help but think opposites often attract in the hope of evolutionary broadening of potential. In any case, two families come together to produce you. You may inherit good or bad traits. You may be a low-down, no-good like your uncle Bob. Each disposition gels over a lifetime. Your plasticity starts like fresh tapioca pudding but hardens into familiarity. You become you, which often reflects an arrangement similar to or dissimilar family. Dissimilarity is probably best characterized in terms of polarity.

Polarity establishes land masses in your psyche. Much of the landmass is territory held in common with others because year after year you govern your mind. Some develop. Let's say your attempt at making New Year's resolutions wanes over the years. It wasn't always so. There were years that it went the other way. You grabbed the bull by the horns. You got fit.

But now, it's been years. This is polarization. Over time you 'freeze' into a disposition.

Polarities are strictures that captivate a way of thinking. They maintain jurisdiction. Not going to the gym is a primal 'thing'. It may well brush up against a genetic thumbprint. A grandparent may have had resolution issues. The gravitational pull can be very strong when current generation and previous generation align.

Before my older brother died he enjoyed his retirement for some years. I'm sure he felt released from his past much as I now feel released from mind. My brother was a rebel. Rebels then were often called bad eggs. It would make sense that my parents might have some turbulence in their first born. Each of them had mothers who died before they were 12. They had haphazard upbringings.

Because of the family structure, my father's fights with his eldest made me timid and afraid. My brother was a guitar-playing, sports guy who took out his insecurities on bullies, fighting guys twice his size. His name was always in the local paper for hockey, lacrosse, baseball. The Chicago Black Hawks invited him to their training camp.

I pumped iron as a teenager but shied away from fighting till I took up boxing at age 26. This could be a latency effect caused by growing up in the shadow of my big brother. A polarity.

My father liked horse radish and gave me a spoonful when I was a kid, then laughed like my reaction was the funniest he'd ever seen. It's polarity that one develops even in one's taste buds. Primal polarities exist in term of fundamental latitude and longitude within the self. We set up defence mechanisms so these polarities don't question themselves.

The constituent factors within our innumerable polarities, big and small, make up our subconscious restraint mechanisms. Before you know you are you your subconscious is quite aware of where you are locating yourself in experience.

Mental health runs askew when polarities don't add up, or collide in dysfunctionality crushing circuitry and with it, put severe dents in primal energy and primal identity. Quite parallel is Einstein's picture of relativity as a bowling ball on a trampoline or net. Major histories and, even more so, major events in your life crystalize into an embrace of life or a rejection in part or as a whole. Total eclipses are serious emotional events. When the heart goes into the blender it comes out as something newly relativized.

Fundamental to our understanding of sociology and psychiatry is the overreaching fact that emotional failure can polarize a person negatively. Once burned, twice shy. A person can become a person who is comfortable in their misery resigned to the place they have in their own narrative. The baggage or burden we carry, the monkey on our backs, is inextricably linked cell to cell and short circuits electricity draining us of energy.

FASHIONABLE MENTAL ILLNESS

I am afraid that we are escalating the very initiatives that form the reality that brings about mental illness. Dislocated in terms of history, depersonalized in terms of function, we are objectively detached in remote-control land out of our own bodies. It gets worse.

We no longer have the collective attention span as something manipulated by coherence. Coherence becomes a challenge in an attention-deficit world. Nobody has time or incentive to bring these machinations to a halt. The human mind is scattered. There seems no way to nail down a truth. The signs that we are losing it are all around us. Mental illness has invaded every street in North America. We have no way out of this madness.

The way we go about business, or justice or education, has a huge down side. Soon it will be impossible to reverse the grain and recapture what is being lost. What is lost is BELIEF.

Never before has so much history washed up on shore of mental vacuity, and never before has history been so bent on repeating itself.

I am, after all is said and done, saying that we, despite our naively great intentions, we the collective have been bushwhacked, hoodwinked and mesmerized into a social fabric that will soon be seen as entirely incapable of mental health. Mental health depends on some cohesive world view. The mentally corrosive nature of where we are placing ourselves, between objective and subjective realms, will become easily our most unsolvable problem.

LEAVE IT TO BEAVER

We have played our way into this reality, simply by growing up, being shoved incrementally from the sidelines into a game that preceded us. Einstein characterizes human birth akin to being born into a herd of stampeding buffalo. We barely have time to catch our breath let alone make a difference. Everybody around us is carrying everything forward. We are part of that everything. We are in the mix, and the mix is in a blender of our own making. Money makes the world go 'round and everybody is passing the buck. It's like a midway ride.

Uncharacteristically and in unprecedented ways, the ground is shifting under us, and does so at an astonishing rate. 'The only constant is change,' is an old saying. What we are dealing with is different; it is change coming with such velocity that we have nothing to which we can anchor the mind except change itself. The speed is like a wind tunnel. It shaves our eyes and ears. Change is no anchor. The result is a society caught in high-paced, highly-bracketed determinism bent on making us all, after all the other stuff is said and done, mentally inefficient at dealing with it. What must be dealt with is phenomenological. It is experiential. It is emotional. We only have mental coherence if our existent emotional needs don't get twisted. A psyche that turns on itself is a dreadful thing.

Once we fail to have sufficient grounding in self-understanding we lose track of what it takes to be who we are. When coherence can't put a drawstring around our thinking in any convincing way and pull it tight, the mind is well on its way to being lost. Most don't know where to gather themselves. Calibrated indices of experience never have the chance to add up to us. Our self-definition lags behind our activities. We have to live with never measuring up to what we once hoped to be. That is devastating for many.

FUTURE SHOCK

Future shock is so exciting, sending us about, sparring with phones and iPads, that we barely recognize the shock. The shock is in the brain; the speed it works at to digest the crap you put it through. The pace is palpably different. Future shock is daily occurrence. In a technological world, overbite is the price of admission to learning curve. Nowhere in history has the human brain gone full tilt boogie into sensory overload such as current technological interface dictates. You are losing your mind because there isn't enough mind to go around.

The subject is bigger than you. Mind is put through a digital strainer. You have no time to gather yourself. Self loses its sense of being referential except in terms of being elbow to elbow with everyone else. You can't see the forest for the trees. It's an old idea with a brand new meaning that Marshall McLuhan articulated with precision. HOT-COLD-HOT-COLD. Our minds are orchestrated by a technology grafted to our central nervous system. That makes it as central as central gets.

This electronic universe is an extension of our central nervous system, and what turns us on turns us off eventually. We are victims of thresholds. We are irrevocably massaged and invaded by a hot-cold media-controlled sequencer, embodying a past-went-that-away reality. The bottom line: we can't catch up with ourselves. That creates discontinuity in how we become who we are and enormous problems in how we feel about ourselves.

In the old days families would make preserves. Jams and pickles and relish and the like would be sealed for future use...to be pulled from the pantry shelves in the thick of winter. There is a fitting analogy here. Currently, every day we stack the shelves of our mental outlook. Each day runs into the next. Shelves are stocked and consumed as one thing replaces the next in its contextual immediacy. Everything is dictated by a predisposition to an energy-desperate ongoingness, an ongoingness, directed by polarization of persona and of gratification, dictating threshold worthiness, excluding all else. All else includes deep thought and evolution of sensibility. The bottom-line is that your predisposition arrives before you do. Your thresholds have organized.

SANITY

This is hardly a recipe for a successful book: telling people they better be very careful how they stack their brain shelves. But that's what this book is about. A lapse here and there and the brain you know too well will give up the ghost. You have heard of pathological liars. All mental illness is pathological. It comes about because we miss subtle clues about the big questions as to how we are modelling ourselves. Our refusal becomes pathological, part of a defense system with rigidity and refusal built into our cellular polarity. We build ourselves into blindness and emotionally and, all too often, feel prey to predispositional character armour.

One cannot ignore social gravity. The world is headed in a certain direction so history tells us. What is truly weird is how we graft to history so easily knowing where it is all going. Just because we are afraid to face ourselves. To keep a leg up on the future, we have to be up to our neck s in it. For perspective this is less than ideal.

We don't learn because we can't. We are literally schooled to unlearn the things that make us most human. The arts amplify us, science objectifies us. We fill ourselves with information on the amber-alert world and its needs and this dictates learning trajectory according to, what else but, economic viability. There are no free rides. Get your nose to the grindstone. The early bird gets the worm.

This is the only message that gets through to youth: that they must earn their keep. No longer is morality taught. No longer is solitary fun an option. Like religion it is passé, trumped by objectivity and science and the concomitant dog-eat-dog reality of survival of the fittest. We no longer live within self-concepts that nurture who we are, simply what we can become as earners, in this or that job market. The adventure of life becomes less inviting.

PLATO'S CAVE

It couldn't be more evident, I believe, that our world is imploding from lack of sound leadership. This distills down to all levels of society. Plato believed a country should be run by philosopher-kings because philosophers aren't captivated by greed and hence they don't need the cash cow so esteemed by contemporary politicians. Greed, for a philosopher, is an impurity; it is a poison that can take over a man's mind. To believe a mansion can make you empowered is literally oppositional to what a philosopher sees as true empowerment. For a philosopher, a man who needs a mansion to appear powerful is simply a 90 pound psychological weakling. He's been tricked by eyeball glitter and artificial status. A man with the 'display' of success about him is acting out of defensiveness. This is a man profoundly insecure. He needs his skyscraper, jet, trophy wife and limo to establish self-hood. Without a gold-plated crutch he can't stand the flack.

That's why this book, which is essentially about the brain, needs to reference the world as it is. The world as it is shapes us fires and wires our brains.

We need to come to terms with the forces that impinge upon us. Everything comes down to how our brains deal with this massive interface. There is nothing more important than your world view because in that world view is a character, namely you, who is trying to sort life out.

You are walking through your narrative. You have a script. Some of the script you get to write, some was handed to you.

These are dangerous times. If you've grown up in a small community as I did, you begin to recognize a startling fact...that many of the now-demented, were once seemed to be pillars of strength in the community. Is there a connection between material success and mental decay? Does material success demand so much outward bound energy there is no inward bound energy?

I occasionally see pictures in the paper of guys I went to school with who now own the town.

I should look at them and respect their accomplishments, but I see it as sad...to get trapped in this ideation of self simply out of lack of whatever to entertain existential challenge beyond the incubation of their small town destiny, and the nature of its perceived ambitions and obvious rewards.

LIPSTICK ON MY COLLAR: EGG ON MY FACE

The brain ultimately does value appearances. We put on a face on to meet the faces that we meet. We get lost in the image-making machinery. That's why we buy lipstick and tooth whitener and wrinkle cream and own the latest iPhone. We pass ourselves off as a package. It makes for a fragile and vulnerable self.

A brain with inner strife lacks co-ordinated effort. A few bonfires in the cortex, the amygdala and the hippocampus, can cause contradiction within localized firing and wiring realities. The brain is the house you live in. A house divided cannot stand. Just like athleticism helps the body stay active, athleticism in the mind helps the mind to stay agile. Most people have an agile frontal cortex; the mind-forged manacles are here. Like the Canada Arm, the nature of reach is designed within attention span reality. This area is so bullish it forgets everything beyond its agenda. The rest of the brain, far from being agile, is sluggish. Brain atrophy begins in the unused brain and spreads eventually to the 'used' brain. Sudoku and crosswords and brain training won't do anything for the right brain where big picture coherence happens.

To be a couch potato in the corpus callosum, or amygdala while your frontal cortex does it all, is a recipe for a disaster. Discontinuous mental activity creates a disorganized mindscape. Working memory shrinks and long term memory disappears. Watching your life pre-eminently with the frontal cortex and its parallax bracketing creates distortion, including numbing levels of acceptable levels of dissociation. This is the sort of dissociation a TV set engenders going from tragedy to flickering commercials.

A left brain mind is a mind with precision and exactitude. But beyond this application of practical no-nonsense formatting is a profound subjectivity, a huge motif that must be addressed. We need the left brain to satisfy our need to be rational. We cannot go it alone with the left brain and feed our essence without the more intangible elements like creativity and right brain, big picture, orientation. When your brain tries to settle down and sleep, it can't satisfy coherence when a million unattended fires are burning out of control.

Try as it might, your dream consciousness can't rescue a useable idea of you if you are running into the future. Night after night it coughs up cutting floor bits and pieces. It is here the rebellion against being you first rears its ugly head. The orchestrated brain makes sure the violins, the horns and the kettle drum all have input. The brain's complexity demands a finely tuned orchestra. Anything unused atrophies. It doesn't go down without a fight though. It may be ignored, but it's not forgotten. The mind has a mind of its own. It will rear its ugly head.

FLYPAPER

Only one year in my teaching career did I have to teach the novel, Lord of the Flies. I didn't like the novel because it was difficult to get past the plot.

The title of the book should provide an overriding clue; that this is a cautionary tale. When things are out of hand all that is left are the flies buzzing around decomposing things.

In the end brute force barbarism, wherever it happens, ends up the same, in push-comes-to-shove carnage everywhere. It is formulaic, it is historical.

What does it mean to be lord of the manor if that entails being lord of the flies?

Despite the cautionary tale aspect of the novel, few questioned its premise in this respect. Most students took it for granted that without civilization's doily tablecloths and pleasant valley Sunday political correctness, the human would waste no time reverting to the beastliness. It was, they thought, a foregone conclusion; that away from the parents, the motivation for civilization would cease. Piggy, who had his glasses broken, was the only who could see the big picture. The others wanted no part of restraint; they wanted no part of the big picture.

Empathy in a world of anti-empathy: THAT IS THE DEFINITION OF THE FUTURE.

"The point is, these capitalists – they and a few lawyers and priests and so forth who lived on them – were the lords of the earth. Everything existed for their benefit. You – the ordinary people, the workers – were their slaves. They could do what they liked with you. They could ship you off to Canada like cattle. They could sleep with your daughters if they chose," (George Orwell, Nineteen Eighty-Four, p. 75).

How many people know Canada was mentioned in 1984?

Where society is going has a lot to do with how you feel about the plight of others. Refugees coming across the Canadian border from the U.S. are often hated by the same people who applaud themselves for Canada's Underground Railway delivering Blacks from oppression. This is what today's version of the Underground Railway looks like.

In 1984, Winston struggles with empathy.

"A curious emotion stirred in Winston's heart. In front of him as an enemy who was trying to kill

him: in front of him, also, was a human creature, in pain and perhaps with a broken bone. Already he had instinctively started forward to help her. In the moment when he had seen her fall on the bandaged arm, it had been as though he felt the pain in his own body," (George Orwell, Nineteen Eighty-Four, p. 87).

War happens because men can't visualize what life is like with PTSD in a wheelchair. War is about securing some bloody hamburger hill and sticking a flag up the enemy's ass. How brilliant. How juvenile!

By shuffling the deck constantly, by calling real news fake news, and fake news real news, Donald Trump is opening Pandora's Box. Where does the future go after Trump has taken out the key game pieces? If you can't ascertain truth you can't ascertain enemy.

Trump is not the subject of this book. I'm making a sociological point. The state of the nation weighs heavily on us all and demands our brain activity. Donald Trump is a force on the planet just as the media is a force. Reality is a force in our brains.

SOAP BOX DYNAMICS

Soon, only local news with a local circumference will be trustable. Maybe not even that. In Canada we don't know our neighbours, generally speaking. We would have no idea as to whom a microphone should be given if a local catastrophe occurs. At the point, where conventional truth is broadsided, as In Orwell's 1984, the truth breaks down. As Sinead O Connor put it, to speak the truth is to dig your own grave. There is no choice other than falling victim to information. Everything becomes a mental phenomenon. As such, it is as intangible as the air we breathe. We become weary of untruths but incapable of discerning real truth. Confused, we need something simple, a simple idea or slogan. Real truth becomes narrowed down to opinion.

Knowing where things are at is to recognize we are reaching critical mass in socialization issues and, frankly, things are becoming treacherous.

I don't think this is hyperbole. Like Doublethink and Double Speak described by Orwell, the principles are simple enough. Squeeze the human brain between two opposite poles and what you get is a brain plasticized to see alternative truths as equally viable. Once you say, with equal interest and disinterest, that 2 plus 2 equals 4 and 2 plus 2 doesn't equal 4, you have the camera of the mind tied in an optical mental knot. At this point, 2 plus 2 equals whatever, it's just a number.

Rational, logical thought has no basis once this is the case. It only took Trump eighteen months to upset the American apple cart. So the mind doesn't give up under the weight of this confrontational fundamental inconsistency in ourselves; we need alternative ways of processing thought. How do we format a mind not so easily messed with? How do we recognize our complexity without being overwhelmed?

71

SIX TOES AND MORE

In John Wyndham's novel, The Chrysalids, the kids are alright with communicating over vast distances via thought-shapes. Thought shapes seem familiar to those who configure their own thinking. It is, indeed, the very shape of overall thought that creates communication that naturally transcends rote verbalization. Trying to say what we mean by reducing it to words can be tricky. Indeed, our predicament is only assailable by analogy.

We can embody so much in analogy, which is a kind of thought shape with moving parts.

FREEDOM IS SLAVERY

Verbalization can trap us. In 1984, Orwell tells how the word 'free' is still in use in the new dictionary, in respect of a dog being free of fleas or someone being free of debt. But 'free' in a sense of political freedom doesn't exist in the new dictionary. It is without dictionary support. It is dead to language usage. By curtailing language one curtails thought.

The entrapment of the under-educated American mind is fait accompli. The way America is set up it's a slam dunk. A simple slogan like **_Make America Great Again_** they can understand. Other countries are aghast that Americans have sunk so low so quickly. Where did the ignorance come from? Where did all their intelligence go? Where did all this stupidity come from if not manufactured at home?
What is it about America's News and Entertainment that made them an easy touch?

A big part is an education system taken over by big time sports. Schools are run for their sports program. No academic criteria respect the true reality of evolving thought. There is no oversight of conceptual growth. For America it's MBA or the highway. Education is nickeled and dimed, and moth-balled.

It's from a different era that America established itself. Harvard and Yale are dishing up the same scope as any institution of higher learning anywhere in America. Mediocrity is everywhere. The half-time show is so pervasive, the university presidents make a fraction of what stadium-filling coaches get. America has fallen victim to its own RAH RAH RAH. God is great. Money is God.

Of course, it comes from values attributed to certain things and unattributed to others. It comes from people who think having a female soccer team in Iran (profiled in an Anderson Cooper documentary) is some kind of salvation. This is the great American homogeneity; that everyone participate in the same stupidity-laden reality and everybody will be happy.

How farcical that Americans are so ignorant. What else, for God's sake, could happiness consist of, than playing soccer, baseball or whatever?

Everywhere it's a game of Kings and Little ones. The Kings make the rules. Business 101. They pay the price. Sports as salvation? - I don't think so.

Much of the mental decline in America can be attributed to the ascent of sports programs paralleled with the demise of art programs and creative non-competitive community outlets.

Sports are the only game in town for the budding youngster. Sports nurture an idea that all is good if people let off steam through their athleticism. Then you go share a couple of beer and talk about it. It symbolizes the most basic and simple reality: physical prowess trumping physical prowess. Body transcending mind. What other scale of events could be better?

RED LINING RED SQUARE

Leaks from security insiders point to pre-presidency, under-the-table, communication with Russian officials. Can you imagine how scandalous this would have been in the McCarthy years when every communist was being hauled out of their jobs, into witch-hunt court rooms everywhere? So Trump is smart in bringing up McCarthyism before his opponents bring it up. He defaces truth by identifying his actions in terms of shuffling distractions.

Once upon a time, people would have called this so-seeming connection with Russia treason.

THE REAL BOMB: WHEN RUSSIA WAS RUSSIA

It should be mentioned that years after the fact Americans would indeed learn about collaboration with the Russians.... that since 1943, the soviet intelligence had been receiving periodic progress reports on the bomb. In the McCarthy years, America suffered from what was officially labelled Security Syndrome. The very odour of Ruskie information got them so paranoid, so running around like chickens with their collective head cut off, they were tossing big time heroes like Oppenheimer under the bus. McCarthyism demonstrates the infinite reliability of reducibility of the human mind to 2 plus 2.

A recent book, America's Best and Brightest (2017), shows how blinded the American military was by fear of Communism, and especially by its own arrogance setting off a chain of stupidity of staggering proportion in Vietnam.

Turns out the best and the brightest were mental midgets. This is the point of plasticity. Your capacities are attributable to design motifs. So what is smart when stupid is what stupid does?

"In most scientific circles, the excommunication of J. Robert Oppenheimer from government service is regarded as the nadir of his country's superstitious quest for absolute safety. But the case is more than a pathological specimen of the operation of the American security system, (Gerald Dickler, editor, Man in Trial, p. 376).

Oppenheimer's case represents the consummate pathology of fear blinding interrogators to facts. Oppenheimer went from national hero as head of the Manhattan Project to national zero for no other reason than America-brand, self-inflicted, popular paranoia.

And to top it off, his mother was an artist, and they had an art collection....absolute crimes against humanity. Art was considered a weapon of mass destruction.

Security Syndrome was the name attached to the face of America at this time. The collective pathology was concrete in its obsessions.

An unresolved subconscious makes the persona act out in ways of defined contours. Narrowing the mind, to gateway the intellect, is pre-set territory, so ambiguities are squeezed out of the picture. It becomes a beast bent on chasing, then eating, its own tail. This is what simple slogan language is all about and the shape of the mentality thereby manifest. The very people disenfranchised by Trump-Care were the suckers who voted for him.

The American mind is primitive, propaganda-driven, patriot-loving, mental midget gadgetry with its own wind-up principles. Not without an array of trigger-happy understandings concocted on the basest of materials. He's proud of it. Better be a dumb-ass patriot than a commie lovin' bastard. America lives in a blind spot. A week ago, our Prime Minister Justin Trudeau was referred to as Joe Trudeau by the White House Spokesman. How do you have credibility when sovereign states barely register on the nameplate?

You don't need sophisticated smoke and mirror props and a special effects crew to snowplow the human mind. The human mind is there for the taking. That leaks are more important than the substance of the leaks can be revelatory in characterizing a society doomed by its own hand.

Journalists don't distinguish here between substance and news. News in any shape or form is ratings. Collusion with Russia over sanctions and interference in the American election should shake the very foundation of a nation's self-understanding. But Trump and his red necks are oblivious to anything complex and conscientious. Like the Proles in 1984, short of a bomb falling on their heads, they savour their political ignorance. They demand it.

BASKET CASE

In the news, the small and the large are handled routinely for their hot potato optics. Apples and oranges are tossed indiscriminately in one basket.

This morning on CP24 news, the morning crew laughed their fool heads off at a goat falling down, perhaps getting injured. What's funny about that? The other morning launch item on this station, was a letter written by a girl to her boyfriend who subsequently red-marked the mistakes, circling grammatical errors. So much of our humour is descriptive of a highly-tuned insensitive society, a society so routinely cruel it has lost all bearings. It loves itself for what it can make trite.

Candice Wiggins, in retiring from the WNBA, cited the reason as toxic environment. Women are trying to bully their way into prime time intrigue all entirely based on the premise: you have to have balls. Having balls means bullying.

Years ago, tennis player Serena Williams hurled some very ugly expletive deleted-s at a female umpire who, I believe, had innocently enough, called Serena for a foot-fault. It was obvious the startled, diminutive oriental woman, and for that matter, I myself, had never heard such vulgarity leaping from the female

77

mouth. Somewhere around this time, the female locker room in professional women's tennis was a place of vulgarity and intimidation. Women can be mean bastards just as much as male counterparts. Many feel called upon to establish their 'male' oriented strength.

MY HOME TOWN: ORANGEVILLE ONTARIO CANADA NORTH AMERICA

Growing up in my town, in that era, it would be said of so and so that she wears the pants in the family. Maleness is seen in terms of aggressiveness hence characterized as dominating and dictatorial. If the success prototype was etched in different criteria we would have a different social structure and entirely different life-span experience. If intelligence, in terms of human sensibility rather than in terms of money making ability, was the key to success, the whole read-out would be a different read-out.

ANOTHER BRICK IN THE WALL

Schools teach information. They no longer teach students.

"Patience is a student's great virtue; it is the mark of the best quality of mind. It takes an eternity to unfold a universe; man is the sum of the achievements of innumerable ages....the will to know, manifesting itself in persistent impulse, in never-satisfied yearning, is the power which urges to mental effort and enables us to attain

culture," (J.L. Spalding, Means end Ends of Education, p. 47).

Here is another quote from the same text, a book published in 1903.

"None of us yet know for none of us have yet been taught in early youth, what fairy palaces we may build of beautiful thought – proof against all adversity;- bright fancies, satisfied memories, noble histories, faithful sayings, treasure-houses of precious and restful thoughts; which care cannot disturb, nor pain make gloomy, nor poverty take away from us – houses built without hands for our souls to live in," (J.L. Spalding quoting Ruskin, Means and Ends of Education, p.7).

VIDEO KILLED THE RADIO STAR

To build a deep-seated innerness is hardly easy. Video killed the radio star is now a fact of history in many ways. People who imagine the song when they hear it, often imagine the television video of the song.

Before the video scorched their minds, individuals imagined the song's meaning from scratch, via their own camera, their own internal homegrown response, in their own IMAGINATIONS.

In a sense, our imagination has been irrevocably violated, supplanted by someone else's ideas. When I accompany my wife to functions in the homes of education administrators I see no books. For vast segments of the population books are a foreign substance.

Reading literature is fertile ground for capacitating empathy, understanding, and conceptual growth. Reading happens at absorption speed appropriate for longevity and continuum. The right brain turns black print on a white page into voluminous accounts in reflective visual projections, complete settings that are firmly lit in a digestible context. The big part of innerness and the imagination is an exercised firing and wiring of cathartic identification. Deepness in our culture has been eroded by superficial gambles for the carcass of the dark knight's darkness, and the human condition is no longer showing up at the table in anything close to peak condition. The eroded mindscape is easy pickings for mental illness or shifty slick politicians with graphic soothers in tow.

The point of education is to raise us above where we would be without it. If someone is alienated, dazed and confused, so often the need is human intervention; a helping hand is a million times more strategic than information. The inclination in our society is towards a superman dictatorship...anything else is too inconvenient, too confusing for us for whom thinking is an antique.

THE GONG SHOW

It's easy to be hard and make fun of others. From the Gong Show to contemporary reality, TV partakes of the vicarious cruelty that makes people pee their pants in disbelief. That, in this day and age, as per the CP24 story, someone took the time and effort to write a letter, a real live handwritten letter, means they should be heralded, not held up for scorn. To not be swept up in this vicarious cruelty is a problem. It is an incremental challenge. Eventually viewers will find people walking into a gas chamber hilarious, all because of the infinite, but incremental, divergence. It's so easy to forget to remember where we once were.

DOWN WITH BIG BROTHER

Winston, in Orwell's 1984, is wondering if anyone besides him detects the lies and manipulation. Does anyone remember anything to compare the present to?

"Being in a minority, even a minority of one, did not make you mad. There was truth and there was untruth, and if you clung to the truth even against the whole world, you were not mad," (George Orwell, Nineteen-Eighty-Four, p. 173).

There will always be puppets looking for the puppet master. **Some people want to use you some want to be abused: Eurhythmics.** It doesn't make Sadism or

Masochism right. Our psychological entanglements abuse our mental health.

Give a person a role to play and they feel like they've been chosen in a game of pick-ups. Without a role we are outcasts.

One of the mottos of Big Brother's society is the slogan: Freedom is slavery. When you are a slave you don't need to figure things out. It wouldn't make any difference, if you did. The Master is going to call the shots. Life is taken care of. This is precisely why Eric Fromm wrote Escape from Freedom. For with freedom comes responsibility of the self to the self, without the doctrine of some indoctrination to look through. Freedom is terrifying. People who retire can be freaked out by the need to find something different to do with their time. Chronology is no direction. Direction comes from conscience and conscience is ever-evolving.

People will willingly compete to do the soul burglary necessary, and the salute, and the goose-step and the ass-kiss, all in one smooth motion, if you just let them belong. Just give them a name tag and a place at the table.

They have no ethical basis for being and are hence visitors passing through their own mindscape. Entrapped by the day-to-day scandal of being there provides little substance and no continuum of references to sift through. Once you lose your bearings everything starts looking as familiar and unfamiliar as anything else. Most people don't get beyond it-is-what-it-is perspective. You can't hit what you can't see. People like Trump can't conceive of a world without war. Those who can, shudder at such stupidity.

Salvation could be just round the corner inside your self, but you'd never find it. Everybody is in their bubble pretending there is no bubble.

Everything the education system does has little to do with learning. Similarly, the legal system has nothing to do with justice. These are the realities well-entrenched and well-versed.

As justice sharpens its tools to cut more babies in half, the need for alarm is everywhere. Solomon was confronted by two women arguing the ownership of a child. Fine, said Solomon, we'll cut the baby in half. One of the women shrieked and wise old Solomon knew she was the child's true mother.

Schools not aware of big picture ripple effect cut the baby in half as a matter of course. It's routine. It's protocol. It's boots on the ground reality.

"The law sharpens the mind, by narrowing it Justice Oliver Wendell Holmes once said," (Gerald Dickler, editor, Man on Trial, p. 1).

Narrow minds are minds that sort things out in terms of a narrower base of criteria. What one gains in efficiency one loses in respect of big picture justice. Justice has to be a big picture item. Narrow minds are a curse.

"The increasing emphasis on 'security' as distinguished from 'loyalty' gave free play to vicious hearts and narrow minds," (Gerald Dickler, editor, Man on Trial, p. 385).

Eventually, narrowness becomes accelerated and matter-of-fact expediency. It becomes unnoticeable. These are the concomitant realities when process becomes job. When job becomes a series of actions.

This narrowing down of the premises of operation becomes a narrowing of consensus world-wide. By objectifying methodology we objectify people. Human Resource makes people into Widgets. When policing has nothing to do with fairness, youth have no choice between good and bad. Bad for them is cops. **Cops cause crime** because they are, in many cases, crime advocates. They rub people the wrong way.

The neighbourhood is on edge when the Gang of Blue pushes everyone around. It stresses everyone and makes for a lot of contempt and hatred. A stressed society is a violent society.

HANDS UP

The Toronto police have a billion dollar budget. Giving that money to community centres, youth programs, and culture and learning initiatives would give ten times the bang for the buck in terms of positive social adjustment. The cost of alienating large segments of ourselves creates insurmountable friction and inescapable debt.

The art world has gone through this same criteria narrowing. They no longer have any self-concept initiatives that have anything to do with creativity and originality. They are their own brand. They are afraid of making mistakes so they continue to rubber stamp mediocrity and make the world yawn. Defensively, they cast disparaging glances from their ivory tower niches, fiddling while Rome burns.

Art is dead. Where's the Funeral? That's my next book.

Identity comes at a higher price, in this technological world, where there is no time with sufficient gathering features to devote the necessary courage to anchor oneself. Your mind is a garden, but if all you do is water the plants in the front yard, the frontal cortex, you are dying elsewhere. A mind full of weeds gets entangled in itself. With fleeting mind we face an information barrage like never before. We are stressed. Fight or flight is superimposed into each and every moment.

Behaving as the wind behaves; we recognize there is no way of leveraging our thoughts into the game. We are disenfranchised by the world's power structures.

**Our dried voices, when
we whisper together
are quiet and meaningless
as wind in dry grass
or rats feet over broken glass....lips that
would kiss**

Form prayers to broken stone. ....T S Eliot: The Hollow Men

We are stuffed with the circuitry, the stuff of generations before, compacted together and repacked for deployment. Our kisses form prayers to broken stone. Whatever solid truths proclaimed as necessary in the stories of humankind we have forsaken. Stuffed with affluence, hollow of meaning, there is uneasiness within any level of thoughtful discernment. The American alcoholic, who calls the shots in America (usually on the ninth hole), is many more times, than in the rest of the world, likely to be hooked on prescription pain killers and anti-depressants. Between upper and downers there's barely time or energy to set the house in order. When it comes to the brightest of the military bright lights, you are talking about anti-conceptual, anti-intellectual bird brains. The only ideas with traction are age-old ideas. The intelligence mustered here on the battlefield of ideas and allegiance is that of eight year olds in a sandbox. The uniformed Generals Trump surrounds himself with are schooled in their schooling. They cannot transcend that. They look surprisingly like the Nazi uniforms of days gone by.

SEE DICK JUMP HIGH

Most people can't read what this book, the one you are currently reading, entails. Give yourself a pat on the back. People can read words, but those words for most people don't make it past the popular motif configurations. See Dick run.

Indeed, people have never had reason to learn in their education what tiers of literature exist and what they convey about the psychiatric dimensions of reality. Unfortunately, this makes one ill-equipped for any altitude in their own mental topography. Sanity cannot be found on the merry-go-round of things put on your plate to distract you long enough to sell you something. The formatting and organizing principles of Mind-Set preclude who we are and how we are likely to think. Analogy, metaphor and allegory need to be taught as conceptual devices. We need to embody learning, not enfranchise information.

Winston in Orwell's 1984 describes how short-circuited people are:

"It includes the power of not grasping analogies, of failing to perceive logical errors, of misunderstanding the simplest arguments if they are inimical to Ingsoc, and of being bored or repelled by any train of thought which is capable of leading in a heretical direction. *Crimestop*, in short, means protective stupidity...the key-word here is *blackwhite*....This word has two mutually contradictory meanings. Applied to an opponent, it means a habit of impudently claiming that black is white in contradiction of the plain facts. Applied to a Party member, it means a loyal willingness to say that black is white when Party

demands this....This demands a continuous alteration of the past, made possible by the system of thought which really embraces all the rest, and which is known in Newspeak as *doublethink*," (George Orwell, Nineteen-Eighty-Four, p. 173).

Sanity is so taken for granted in America they are at a loss to figure out the fraying of the social fabric. America is teetering on civil war - Muslim versus so-called Christian, Black versus White, Rich versus Poor. They are only a hop, skip and a jump away from minor incidents triggering civil war. First it will be L.A., then New York, then everywhere. Just like the phrase of the day.

Around where I live, many upstanding businessmen have succumbed to dementia. When, as I've said before, time is money, the accelerator controls consciousness. An accelerated, time-is-money consciousness doesn't grasp anything so much as exploit the moment for business leverage. Consciousness doesn't gather itself around the business man. The expedient businessman has no reason to doubt his life's game plan. It works in the way he wants it to work. It just doesn't work till the end.

Once it truly hits you that you can't take it with you your life conquest is made of less viable stuff than ever thought possible. You don't see it till the carrot in front of your nose disappears.

Looking at virtually comatose patients in an old folk's home is hard to bear. The life force has crashed in these people, in their ability to daily incarnate themselves. The axons and dendrites and synaptic juices have dried up. Neurons have gone to seed.

We are so busy looking in the wrong place. We have to find out what is at work here by probing what sorts of people fall prey to dementia. Dementia is pathological. I believe it's because the wrong formatting choices were made in life. The picture of life was a picture snipped off at the edges. An 8 x 10 glossy picture in an idea of reality that was concocted from the moment you came on the scene.

Even if only for a short time, pre-death, being out of sorts, simply not yourself, day after day, takes a toll. It becomes obvious that you are locked out of yourself. Feeling thresholds, you thought would always be there, painfully don't re-incarnate just because you think they should. A person can be a lost soul the moment they lose their mind. Emotions that could pull them back are no longer there. They have become posed affectations.

Sanity is an assumption connected by default to the majority. Namely being able to cope with arbitrary, sound-bite reality without becoming a wing nut. The bar is pretty low. And it's open till 3 a.m.

Because of what is being routinely neglected in the McLuhan-ized, velocity-laden, sound-bite brain, your version of reality isn't going to get you to the finish line, let alone to the Promised Land. It's going to a blow a tire or a head gasket. There is too much mental fatigue.

If you lose the torch that lights the way you are goners. You will forget how to put on your socks, how to manage going to the bathroom, how to stand up sit down. And it all comes about because you aren't a good fit for yourself.

To fit in, one must conform to the majority. People have built their neurological houses on the sand. Like a love letter washed away by the waves, the waves of onslaught are ripple-effect viable everywhere. Everything is all at once in the Global Village. How do you sort yourself out all at once when all at once is all you know?

FAST FOOD BRAIN

It's every day. It's on your plate. No brain is exempt. Each and every person is ultimately responsible for their own plasticity management. Where you fire and wire and how you fire and wire is going to pay sanity dividends or not. Plasticity, because of the shaping forces, can go awry. Every moment you are cutting a baby in half, or not, and you are that baby. Every day your indifference grows or it doesn't. In the end, you are indifferent to your own insanity and that is a problem.

Words can lead places where people can't go. Most people follow See Jane Jump, See Dick Run. We have been educated to believe that once you can read and write you can read and write, right? If you read crap your brain is … well, you get it.

Because our education system teaches reading and writing as a learning action that culminates as itself, we misuse its purposefulness. Analysis of material in terms of levels of understanding, including synthesis, insight and idea structures isn't there. The high school grad, and even now university graduates, can't pursue complexity.

Unfortunately your brain is outfitted for complexity.
COMPLEXITY IS ITS VERY NATURE.

TOP OF THE WORLD

It's like the Titanic. To keep it afloat you need to know
something about floating. You don't only need people for the
kitchen staff or people to clean the toilets, you need somebody
to steer. You, and only you, are responsible for management of
a 100 billion neuron universe. It is an astoundingly big
operation.

Our eat-and-run, fast-food education creates an 'informational'
simplicity unequal to the challenge, fired and wired with pre-
emptive dumbed-down strategies. These pre-emptive strategies
are great for a while. Students navigate by thinking their way
around, without ever having contact with deep thought.

Kids think they are simply going down the menu choosing
something that grabs them more. And they are absolutely right.
Ultimately, they are exclusive in the genre of thoughts they put
through their minds. The result is an inability to probe deeply on
things human, which inherently requires one to stick around and
size up the challenge, and boot a multi-dimensional response.

That's where we are at. What I am saying about the brain will be
a threat to you if you equate thinking, real thinking, with rocking
the boat. My writing is full of what you could call provocation
and consternation because I am de-authenticating your reality. I
am de-authenticating our reality. Your original self is a script
that concludes your mental organization. It announces you.

To get here, above my previous mental organization, to this bird's eye view, I had to de-authenticate myself. That's the transformational aspect of being born again. The point is quite simple. You have only one life to live and you want the best possible life. That entails turning your back on those features of existence that habitually ensnare and polarize your negatively.

I am saying that sanity comes only from right brain, big picture moment to moment rigor, in a brain that banks self-awareness, and holds true to compass-monitoring reminders.

Monitor and mitigate. To stick to your guns, fantasizing your left brain has it all under control, is to make a fundamental error. A brain that tries to hide inside its earlier compass is a brain that eventually will be found out.

DOA

I'll tell you how dementia happens. People will pull out scrapbook glory day stories; trot them up every day at Tim Horton's or Macdonald's. Stories will be verbatim. The details won't be misfiring. It's the spaces in between the memories that are growing abysmally large. Where there could be new firing and wiring there is nothingness. Those stories become spindly little branches in a neural map retreating from knowing who you are. Pretty soon, as conversation pieces, they mean no more than somebody else's story. Then the large spaces in between swallow the bits of cognitive apparatus. These story line fragments are all that is left in terms of energized mental interplay. It resembles an interior monologue overheard by others at designated times. The sad thing is the organizing consciousness simply isn't there. The spaces in the brain dominate the brain.

The ongoingness of the mental decay is never checked because it's not witnessed by the degenerating mind. The mind slipping into dementia keeps an assortment of mental furniture and stage business he or she identifies with, within reach. Then one day, the kitchen table and the bathtub are surrounded by blankness. To escape would be to authenticate a coherent landscape where value is valued beyond the original compass. This is the sole responsibility of narrative. That's why bookstores are full of self-help books. The so-called human progress has been anything but human progress as far as the human psyche is concerned. One needs to seed new firings and wirings to create anti-entropy in the brain.

DOLLY PARTON'S COAT OF MANY COLOURS

Before Kenny Rogers was a Gamblin' man he was in a group called the First Edition which had the song, **I just dropped in to see what condition my condition is in.** I liked that song. It is an apt description of the conditional reality any identity makes us succumb to. Whoever you are and how that plays out is conditional. Jung called it a Complex because our position within our own psyche reflects a complex arrangement of management styles.

It is increasingly the case amongst people in all income brackets that the mind is a dubious event. It is a by-product of experience velocity. You are the only one in a position to manage your 100,000,000,000 neuron universe. BUT YOU ARE MANAGED BY

IT. So it's a process of give and take. Marx said, 'Circumstances make men; men make circumstances.' If you make the right circumstances for the brain to be healthy, you have a healthy brain.

It is mind boggling to think so few problems have arisen in standardized social conditioning. The problems have been there. Now during scratch and sniff scrutiny we invent misgivings. Acceleration of misgivings is now widely apparent. The fact is the brain is malleable. As pace speeds up, its malleability outstrips sustainability. The human race has never before indulged disagreeable information to the extent we see every day. You could have the ultimate makeover, be made 'over' in a few days to believe a totally alternate History, Geography, even Math, and especially Science. He who controls the Media controls the past. He who controls the past controls the future. If a government dictated everything to be otherwise, so nothing else was on the screen, it would be a simple wavelength of time. This is the part difficult to accept, that our brains are that malleable.

If we don't turn education upside down we are destined to learn mental illness everywhere we are.

"Professor H. L. Hawkins, speaking in 1936 before the British Association for the Advancement of Science:

the high cerebral specialization that makes possible all these developments and the

extraordinary rate at which success has been attained both point to the conclusion that this is a species destined to a spectacular rise and an equally spectacular fall, more complete and rapid than the world has seen yet," (Malcolm Ross and John Stevens, Man and his World, p.8).

We are blissfully ignorant of what is happening. We like it whole hog. The mind has not ceased to try to keep an eye out for our best interests; it's we who have failed to look out for our mind's best interests.

The mentality-cancer that has taken shape is ultimately represented by a physiological disposition to an amber-alert world. Amber alert poisons the workplace. Tension filters through our ability to organize any agenda. I worked in a tense education environment. The principal in a school doesn't want to alienate the staff. The Social Committee runs the school's social life and becomes the principal's go-to group. There is an inverse proportion relation between the social circle and viable education initiatives. It's pretty safe to say that any organization is dominated by people who see themselves in that role. The gift of the gab makes the gab follow the path of least resistance. This is why Hawthorne segregated himself from his fellow workers at lunch. He knew one could participate but only at a price. He didn't want to be sent down the drain in a swirl of monosyllables.

These teachers that run the schools are the most superficial teachers generally speaking. Teaching is a sideline, socializing is what they are about. To play their game you have to be as empty-headed as they are. You have to have a lot of TV show nonsense between your ears. Serious teachers have to be tense, because superficial teachers have the principal's ear and define the school's who's in who's out culture.

THE EDUCATED IMAGINATION

The human being needs to be educated in the imagination with due process for creativity and insight if sanity is to prevail. You need to know where Waldo is in the big picture if you are Waldo. Most teachers with intuition and imagination are weeded out of the system, making it impossible for students to grasp anything other than methodologies of information. We need a perspective on self to gauge the innumerable upsetting issues that undermine seriousness, at least where seriousness matters. The puppet strings are in the hands of the handful of puppeteers that throughout society exercise Divine Right.

I've started reading a biography of Pushkin, a Russian writer. Beyond Chekov, my Russian writer familiarity is not expansive. Tolstoy and Dostoevsky have been on my 'books to read' list but they are still there. Pushkin goes to a flagship school set up by the Russian Ministry.

"Teachers were, 'never to allow pupils to use words without clear ideas and in all subjects

were to encourage the exercise of reason,'" (T.J. Binyon, Pushkin A Biography, p. 16).

This commonplace skull drudgery, the sort of rules no one who writes would come up with. You only learn to say when you mean by dancing with words. TS Eliot said you can never win with words. By the time you figure out how to say something it's too late. Words do not happen like arithmetic yet the people who run our schools are big on arithmetic and low on creativity. This was a strict school, very regimental.

"Pushkin met another candidate, Ivan Pushchin – my first friend, friend without price... said Puskin.

Malinovsky's private note on Pushkin read: empty-headed and thoughtless. Excellent at French and drawing, lazy and backward at arithmetic," (T.J. Binyon, Pushkin A Biography, p. 19).

I mention this to demonstrate the lack of perception in today's world and how the exercising of such insight is differentiated in our Facebook world. We have speed dial relationships that aren't face to face where body language isn't even part of it.

Eventually Pushkin's Headmaster was replaced by a more empathic one.

"In a word our director understood that forbidden fruit can be a dangerous attraction,

and that freedom, guided by an experienced hand, can preserve youth from many mistakes...above all he was concerned to establish 'amical relations' between himself and the lycéens, guiding himself by the maxim that 'only though a heartfelt sympathy with the joys and sorrows of one's pupils can one win their love,'" (T.J. Binyon, Pushkin A Biography, p. 23).

Why more people don't throw up their hands in despair or 'go postal' is reflective of the fact we believe ourselves to be in control, a belief soon to be tested by political extremes. It will take only a very little to push people over the edge. It would have been impossible to imagine a couple decades ago that the human being could be ever again cattle-prodded into an unfortunate destiny. I thought we were too smart for that; too advanced.

THE DELUGE AND THE STRAW ON THE CAMEL'S BACK

The micro-management style in the workplace, coupled with the information barrage, is bringing more and more people to their knees. I remember when all commercials were 60 seconds long. On one scene. This appealed to a longer attention span. Since then the attention span is cut up in snippets. Flashes. Now some commercials are only a few seconds long and flash like strobe lights. Last night my wife and I were checking out the starry sky. The neighbour's TV which was 150-200 yards away pulsed like lightning with its constant image change. We are bedazzled, with all the slicing and dicing of information and yet simultaneously we take it for granted.

Once upon a time I aspired to be a writer, now I couldn't care less. Fame is a bowling ball that warps time-space. It is not something anyone should want. Fame chews you up and spits you out on the front pages. I simply feel obligated to get this book out so people can save themselves from the encroaching abyss. I'm not trying to be arrogant. Life as we know it is slipping through our fingers.

As Leonard Cohen sings, **I told the truth; I didn't come to fool you.**

This book is a book that will piss people off. People hate being called foolish. So why set myself up by writing a book people will willfully ignore? Why such audacity that it's me there putting my finger in the dyke? 'Ignorance is strength' is a central idea in Orwell. By maintaining stupidity one doesn't have to challenge oneself. One can hide under the turtle shell nailed together with old perceptions and old ideas. One doesn't need the courage to develop the continuum of resonance necessary for any future where sanity plays a part. It is what it is. GROUP THINK is Group Think. It is the Global Village. It reigns supreme. When GROUP THINK breaks down ---- society as something homogenous, or even recognizable, will never again have enough coherence to go around. Mistrust will be genetic. We will be scavengers.

KEY WEST

A few years back my wife, Christina, her parents and I were on a trimaran speeding from Fort Myers to Key West. The boat's speed produced a stiff breeze and I marvelled at the tumultuous wake. As usual, I was filming. It was sunny and hot and people were in shorts and tank tops and sprawling sunhats. The ride had almost been cancelled because of choppy water.

The first woman to throw up was a very sophisticated attractive woman a few rows ahead. Within ten seconds ten people were in the middle of throwing up.

This is where we are headed. THE GROUP MIND WILL REGURGITATE ITSELF IN A CRISIS OF IDENTITY. It will start innocently then everywhere all at once people will lose it. The Group Mind will lose it.

Coming soon to a theatre near you, but it won't be theatre. It will be real life.

Our schools need spontaneous art programs to allow individuals the required fortitude to make it safely through the Information Age. Many, many, many are cracking up already, before they are even out of grade school. Many are already drugged. By age 24 they are burned out. Life has zapped them and left them toast.

SANCTITY

Sanity relies on a positive filtering response to environmental insecurity, an insecurity perpetually induced by fear and hate. How we manage this is not new. Socrates said, 'Know Thyself.' There is no more complicated thing than that. By cauterizing the self and burying sensitivity and empathy, we supplant the self with a contrived-to-suit-society self. Indeed, we micro-manage the self in a kind of supply and demand fashion. We exploit ourselves. We make promises to ourselves we don't keep.

How do we know what we know? How do we direct our effort to know and to what end? Most importantly, how do we ask ourselves the right questions to maintain enough self-knowledge to keep ourselves sane?

A lot of this has to do with social optics. What do you latch onto in the information live-stream? For example, few will have failed to hear about Dark Matter and how it is necessary to mathematically account for the weight of galaxies. Still, if you are the average couch potato you probably haven't delved too far into Dark Matter. You've let it pass by your window of perception affording it barely any glance at all.

Dark Matter says to us: we live in a false idea of ourselves. We had thought we were closing in on grasping the universe's final slate of secrets. Now, as it turns out, ninety-five percent of the universe is undetectable and for now, un-knowable. This has shaken faith in science. Or it should.

You have string theory loyalists and parallel universe loyalists and on and on. It is all speculative. The fact that so much of what we know, and how much we don't know, has shifted dramatically is lost on the average Joe, still trying (after 100 years) to wrap their heads around relativity, quantum theory, and light's particle-wave duality. These are just a handful of the stoppers preventing science from closing their door. We are baffled and too arrogant to recognize what our most formidable foe is, namely ourselves.

YOU WANT IT DARKER

It's a fact. We know zip about 95 percent of the universe. What we once considered well-lit, isn't.

We've had such a fetish for science since Copernicus. Everyone abandoned religion to jump on the science bandwagon. It seemed the better way. Now science outside Silicon Valley is way down in the ratings. Science has little input into the senses. People still believe in the out-of-date, idea-of-their-own science. Discoveries of a host of new planets and the black hole at the centre of galaxies would once have blown the socks off the general public. No more. Dark Energy can't handle the Dark Knight.

Daily Planet and Discovery Channel seem old hat. We pick and choose our science. We are loyal to the science at sea level at room temperature, but we don't know what that means. After all, it has been confirmed that we humans spring from one ancestral tree and one ancestral couple living in an Eden-like Africa. And we have a big bang that, like God, bedevils our thinking as to where in the hell it came from. What if God tossed the big bang from the palm of his hand, like a toss of dice? There are physicists right now driving themselves insane speculating as to what preceded the BIG BANG. Maybe what was before the big bang was God playing in the sandbox?

What we truly know about ourselves and our universe is testimonial as to where we, as a world full of billions of Earthlings, are truly at. We, the human race -- where are we at? What's the app for that Jack?

It is interesting how the dead brain looks like hardened rubber or plastic. Alive, the brain has the consistency of tapioca pudding. Over a life time it becomes more solidified as function matches the known, becoming more and more enshrined by firing and wiring proclivity. The brain guck becomes, in firing and wiring patterns, an electrical network metamorphosing into confluence of polarizations, big and small.

Just as the galaxies pivot their polarization on a black hole, so too, the brain possesses its organizing incentive in certain prevailing polarities. Proclivity, propensity and possibility are all give and take in the early brain.

When those polarities sink into plasticity and take concrete form they lose fluidity. The access of stimulus and excitatory synapses are predisposed to automatic default mechanisms that shuffle them away. We prune unused neurons daily. Surely the Grail quest and all quests in any story are about this central nature of quest. The rest is conveyance. How could they explain it without morphing the story into something tangible? The Quest for the Quest as an evolutionary concept-really? Who is going to get it? So you embody it in a story. How do you get this idea to survive generations? All mythology illustrates how man is perpetually duped by the same things.

OUT TOLUNCH OUTTOLUNCH

OUT TO LUNCH

What begins as authorized lapses in overall brain orchestration, by habitual firing and wiring leaning in to automaticity, becomes the nearly fully automated brain. On long trips the automated brain can take over and drive for us. It can take over life that way.

The brain gives up because within its chosen frame of reference, its operational parameters, it has secured a firing and wiring entity. It has connected the dots. Job done.

The brain's job is to complete you. When this lapses, there are no more dots to connect. In terms of consciousness, it aspires only to lock itself in a safe room and wait it out. Polarization governs.

"This hypothesized mixture of automatic and controlled processing likely occurs because of the constant repetition of worrisome thinking. Researchers have found that consciousness controlled, with consistency and repetition, can become automatized and executed outside of awareness as self-contained or 'chunked' motor programs (Brown & Carr, 1989). Posner's (1982) review of empirical evidence indicates that complex semantic processing can also become automated....GAD clients can create an automaticity of those linguistic segments. Instead of behavioural performance, worry involved over-rehearsed, chunked,' conceptual programs which, once initiated either attentively or pre-

attentively, can run to completion without input from the controlled processing system," (James W. Pennebaker, editor, Emotion, Disclosure & Health, p. 61).

AUTOMATICITY RULES

That is the key: you are running to completion of an automated program when you run out of mind. That automated program is the part of you with a mind of its own. It runs you. And it will run you down. Like the energizer bunny you will grind to a precipitous halt.

What we need to be worried about is this controlled processing system and to what extent it has a system dedicated to weeding out the things we actually need to know about. There are things we need to know to preserve our essence. An automatically-controlled processor has potential to turn into our unimaginable worst enemy. We have systematically tried to root out our feelings so we could scale reality without getting bent out of shape. The scale of reality has been scaled to this end. That is unfortunate.

Wherever we come from, (I know, Virginia, we come from the womb) they must have large brains because our brains have to downsize to FIT this planetary field. This stuff about square pegs in a round hole, what's that all about?

Maybe, we are guinea pigs, relatively speaking, to bigger brain creatures who want to see how we make out as Earthlings on planet Earth. An experiment in Earth time with constraints fashioned by stupidity. To fit, we undergo a quickening that burns neurons as fast as they come online.

Imagine your life as a cooking stew. Veggies and meat in a broth cooking slowly towards taste fruition.

Time is of the essence and the order the ingredients arrive and amplify taste is important. Life for many is like a stew that hasn't had the proper ingredients. Those ingredients include imagination, intuition, and the exercise of these in amplification of the spirit. An uninspired brain is an automatic brain.

SPIRIT RALLY

Anyone who has weathered a championship season knows the feeling of confidence conjuring the spirit psychological unity as magic. It's intangible but it makes you feel invincible. Playing a team with a larger 'spirit' than yours is uphill stuff. They click together psychologically. They believe in each other. They believe they can win, whatever the time on the clock.

What is spirit?

Soldiers back from Vietnam often found renewed brotherhood in bike gangs The brotherhood of male-oriented fun, is such that men can understand 'love' among comrades.

It doesn't take a big brain to figure out the consequences in battle if your buddies don't execute well in a war zone. Interdependence is a kind of love. If the Enemy has your front you hope somebody has your back.

This 'love' is rarely translated into love of a female. Females are Triple X or Mamas with little in between.

Through their idealization of sexual and physical compliancy in women, the male mind has a distorted (twisted) view of women and what true love, male-female camaraderie can be like. This contextual thought structure pre-identifies a problem that shouldn't be a problem. Weird as it may seem these rough and gruff men are genetically afraid of women. They are terrified of their feminine side because it makes them Gay. Exercising your feminine side (see Jung) is not about being Gay. It's about giving yourself a little slack a little breathing room to let motivational aspects long repressed into birthdom.

A woman can be a Delilah, a Jezebel. In The Army can instil a vision of woman as a Suzy Rotten-crotch. A painted lady and a bottle of wine can exploit a man's feelings and get under his skin and a shady lady can get what she wants (because she is smarter). A woman can bring a man down; make him look like a pussy, make him look like he doesn't belong amongst men. Look at Macbeth after Lady Macbeth gave him the gears. He has so much confusion and consternation he can't sleep: *Macbeth has murdered sleep*. Macbeth has gone from receiving a promotion as a hero to being an on-the-run traitor. A woman can take you to the bottom faster than a speeding bullet.

Areas of thought structure become firmed up over time. Habits of thought mean we think ninety-five percent of the same thoughts every day. Polarities drift like continents into final formation. Your mind, once your ticket to the outside world, can quickly become a daily prison. You can't be anything other than who you are. Who you are frustrates the hell out of you, but you are stuck.

QUEBEC OR BUST

This morning I dropped my wife, Christina, off at an Orangeville school where she was meeting students to take them on a ski trip to Quebec. It was snowing fiercely on the way to town. There were no trucks and the plows hadn't been out. It was 5:30 am and it was dark. You didn't dare let your attention span wander. This was stressful. If I had to monitor my shoulders, neck and frontal cortex it would be obvious. Stress contours would be there.

My mind was under siege by my attention span. Compared to stress levels many people endure on a daily basis, my drive was a walk in the park. In many cases our aperture on experience is crippled by life not giving us any opportunity to evolve beyond the basics. The thing is, you are both important and not important, if we consider the bigger picture, the evolution of the species. You are important because you are an ambassador for change...you might be the one that leads humanity forward, the fish who walks on shore. Who knows? But if your mind is crimped by experience and forces a reality down your throat that you can't digest, you become an enemy of yourself and of evolution.

A mind in disarray creates a depersonalized and disembodied organism. Body and mind are at cross purposes.

The body often contrives to put the mind out of its misery by introducing cancer, diabetes, heart failure, not to mention acute mental disruption, depression, dementia...any one of these will bring the case-closed agenda forward.

The mid-brain seems like an orchestra conductor making the instrumentation throughout the brain harmonize. When parts of the orchestra shut down, the brain is in recession. These ignored parts atrophy to the equivalency of tangled electrical wires. Circuits once viable now short-circuit through weak points in the atrophied brain. This causes plaquing.

Let's try a different analogy...a traffic cop.

Information comes into the brain from the electrified and toxic, McLuhan-ized world. The traffic cop tries to send it here, there and everywhere including the subconscious. However, the velocity outstrips his ability to organize. Everything rushes to the frontal cortex. In our information-bombarded world there is no let up. Places the traffic cop could have helped with digestion regulation are never given a chance.

HELP

Beyond the plaque debate (brains that look like steel wool) common in dementia, is a different aspect. There are RESOURCE cells available to some. Despite equal plaguing, their minds don't break down. There is a feed...a resource beyond the brain that hasn't signed off. At the very least, this is fluid neuroplasticity and neurogenesis testimonial to a brain that still draws on newness. All other factors being equal, the one loop you want to have is virgin newness. What you can access in your brain after it solidifies into self-hood is the crucial quotient when it comes to dementia. A brain that hasn't closed in on itself keeps the fountain head alive.

Moods affect climate and atmosphere. What grows grows, what dies dies according to climate.

This is the case in the brain. Synaptic juices dry up. The axons and dendrites curl up like plants dying without water. A synaptic event which was once an easy leap becomes more like Evil Knievel jumping Snake Canyon. Without a challenging environment the brain settles into itself. Like Pac Man, the synapses assume consumption patterns and self-regulate, doing this below self-awareness. This victory over you by AUTOMATICITY is your undoing. Conditions form waves and dissipate. Like virtual particles, the name of the game, in a velocity oriented world, is gravitational transference of matter as pure medium. But in the end, the intangible web of firings and wirings settles in to more tangible form. This holds coherence in place or fails to hold coherence in place. Synapse structures are welded into virtually incontrovertible structural form. A cognitive therapist will descend on a connection with a welding torch to change thought routes, but it's tricky, one step-at-a-time business. A better solution is to change the climate.

Changing yourself transformationally involves changing the format of your mind which can be done by resonating with things that matter.

Creativity is everywhere at once.

"So we are, by our nature, creators as well. All of us can, and most of us do, create in one way or another. We are undoubtedly at our happiest when creating, however humbly and inconspicuously. (Paul Johnson, Creators, p.1).

The nature of creativity is profiled in the book, Creators on Creating, from which comes the following Maslow quote. This book was a unique study of creative personages from all walks of endeavour.

"Thoughts like these lead you to the realization that creativity is the most hopeful source of transformations for the good of all. It can bring changes for the better in our own families, our workplaces, our streets, our cities; we ourselves, as creative individuals, can make these changes happen. It is no exaggeration at all to say that creativity is the key to a more advanced humanity, a key to the realization of human potential and the control of human destructiveness," (F. Barron, Creators on Creating, p. 1).

What these quotations describe so well is the dovetailing of creativity and human harmony. When a person gets excited by the creative process they get excited about life.

F. Barron quotes Abraham Maslow, "My feeling is that the concept of creativeness and the concept of the healthy, self-actualizing, fully human person seems to be coming closer and closer

together, and may perhaps turn out to be the same thing," (Creators on Creating, p.1).

Creativity has been a distorted subject area, too frequently confused with invention for profit. It is rather a casual life-long affair of playfulness. Freeman saw a plate rotating in the cafeteria and it intrigued him. It was, as pointed out in the quotation at the start of this chapter, a purely fun thing to think about.

"Creativity is the specifically human resource. It is part of the general human potential, something that we can cultivate in ourselves if we set out to. It is also something that can be nurtured in others who are close to us and perhaps in our care. Teachers can help foster creativity in students, parents and children, and children and parents," (Frank Barron, Alfonso Montuori, Anthea Barron, editors, p. 5).

What is most appreciative of the newest ideas on creativity involves its intangible fluid nature. How could it in its descriptions be so much like the descriptiveness we apply to NEUROGENESIS and NEUROPLASTICITY? CREATIVITY IS PLASTICITY AND PLASTICITY REMAINS THE SOURCE OF SANITY.

No longer is this seen as being undetectable and indeterminable. Neuroscience is profiling creative states and determining their un-deterministic nature with different interpretation outside the paradigm of the more typical standardized scientific exploration. Creativity jumps fences.

The song Yellow was called yellow because there were yellow pages in the room. The movie, Into the West, an exquisite, mystical film, was conceived after seeing a horse on an apartment balcony. The musical, Hamilton, was also by pure chance, having been inspired by a casual choice of a book to read on vacation. Give chance a chance is the creativity motto. The creative mind isn't lockstep with the practical but expansively fishes for connections.

Chance happens everywhere. Everywhere, it is the nature of creativity to free-associate on a larger scale within a synchronicity contradistinctive to logistics that defines itself going forward. The ability to fuse discordant notions together demands a fluid arrangement with one's thinking. Incongruences are there to cross-pollinate.

Creativity and synchronicity enliven our internal space creating a culture, a sensitivity to culture, a sensibility. Creativity helps us converse symbolically and entrain ourselves sub-symbolically. Doing the math no longer means trying to make information that is un-explicit explicit, it means discovering more about the nature of the un-explicit. This is Wittgenstein's mysticism. Wittgenstein was the greatest mathematician to walk the face of the Earth. He knew there is no equation for the perplexing and paradoxical nature of humans. The science behind dating logarithms proves this.

In the writing about sub symbolic processing systems and symbolic processing systems, this book edited by Pennebaker is a beacon in the night. The book entitled, **Emotion, Disclosure, and Health,** ties together creativity and emotional disclosure in terms of mental health. This is especially so in chapter 7, Emotional Attention, Clarity and Repair: Exploring Emotional Intelligence using the Trait Meta-Mood Scale (Salovey, Mayer, Goldman, Turvey, Palfai).

In this book we find out about subterranean demands. I'm not sure what PDF signals are here, but the explanation involving the need to profile our implicit, continuous dimensions of self in a non-classical, knowledge format is strategic to the types of understandings currently surfacing in research. More and more, the unconscious is implicated in our intuition and fulfills analogy as a unique primary process outside left brain chronology.

"In the current research on subsymbolic PDP formats (Rumelhart et al., 1986), complex constructs are being developed , really for the first time, that account systematically for the types of intuitive and implicit processing that analysts associate with unconscious and primary process functions, that have eluded classical information processing models. Subsymbolic processing operates with rapid and complex computations on implicit continuous dimensions, based on principles that are analogic and global,

without formation of discreet categories and without explicit metrics," (James W. Pennebaker, editor, Emotion. Disclosure, & Health, p. 96).

In the end it is our global brain, not our isolated frontal cortex responsible for sanity maintenance.

"In information processing terms, symbols are defined as discreet entities that refer to or represent other entities, and may be combined in rule-governed ways, so that a vast, essentially infinite set of meaningful combinations may be generated from a finite set of elements….Symbols may be images or words; the major processing distinction within the symbolic formats is between nonverbal and verbal forms," (James W. Pennebaker, editor, Emotion. Disclosure, & Health, p.97).

The very things that our left-brain thinks of us can't help but interest us as viable. We, the human species, prefer the tangible and discard creative interplay routinely. Of course, narrative probability cycles allow us to sort out some dimensionality of free-float creativity.

Many artists have given glimpses to us of the way they see things. "**Why shouldn't people agree on the value**

of a work of art as easily as, say, the correctness of an algebraic equation?" (R.M.Restak, The Brain: The Last Frontier, p. 193).

This is always a problem. Hopefully, someday there will be FMRI units at galleries to allow us to investigate the lateral sensibility in art. This is the point with art. Most people would look at Eliot's, The Waste Land, and see it as so much gibberish. Increasing your academic association with art may actually downsize the sensibility experience. This is why art circles are so out to lunch. They circumvent sensibility, confining it to a stratified expectancy, then fortify their opinion masquerading it as fact. A couple coats of veneer and no one knows the difference. One physicians oneself within an academic discipline and that becomes the port hole to tomorrow.

Magnetic resonance as a display of response would establish the complexity of art; its all too often   paradoxical and perplexing nature. You aren't supposed to solve a piece of art like an equation. You are supposed to work with it in your educated imagination.

The industrialized art community has eclipsed these notions by cataloguing styles as if they are constituted by logic. Here is the dichotomy. Ninety-nine percent of art groups, like the Harper Valley PTA, have their partiality strictures. The most profound art comes from discovery in process not from finite actions. On TV I've seen Britain's National Portrait painting contest. The one with the most accurate likeness wins. This is the simplicity that has common-denominator association. Everybody, however lame-brained, gets the meaning of likeness. Psychological portraits don't fly in the British upper crust circle. They are afraid psychology will mess up the experience.

What is Realism? Wouldn't realism be more real if we painted the constituent reality behind the skin like an anatomist's picture of muscles and nerves?

Or more real if we painted a physicist's concoction of arranged molecules?

Vincent Van Goh painted several self-portraits. Each one is a different person; Vincent as dapper, Vincent as monk, Vincent with his ear cut off...one happy, one a little more concerned. Which portrait would win a contest? Of course the question is absurd. When evaluators rule out psychological expressionism in favour of the photographic depiction they should be sent to read the volumes that have been written about the intellectual shortcomings of such method. In my neck of the woods artists are just like this. For them the art wars were never fought. They surrender to the lowest common denominator.

THE DROP OF PROVERBIAL PUCKS

Often a critic will praise something that is way out there, but even then it is outrage in brackets. This involves stuff like the embalmed shark, Richter's grey paintings, and the roller strip of paint at the Canadian National Museum. No wonder the public has issues with an art world that has lost its way. Stupidity like this undermines the comprehension art is so capable of.

It makes one think there is no difference between art they despise and art they shouldn't despise. The most despised art is Surrealism. The 30 minute cake-mix local artist is never so lost as when confronted with Surrealism. They hate it. Their subconscious cannot stand the confrontation.

One recognizes a sunset that was absorptive, or a waterfall, or a time when dead on your feet you crashed on a bed only to find yourself in that hypnogogic state between sleep and wake....spaced out.

Art should absorb us. The religious profess that their belief helps lighten the burden because the burden is in range of perspective, passing through channelled filters that allow absorption in a meaningful way. Art similarly tries to allow us the freedom to make sense of life's travails. What pilgrim would expect smooth sailing all the way? What Quest is without its challenge?

OFF MY CHEST

Indeed, immune system response strength increases when people write things down and get them off their chest. Cortisol levels go to zero when an autistic child spends an hour on a horse. Person-to-person consternation entraps us all. Anxiety is contagious. Alleviation is freedom from consternation. Love alleviates the need to be searching for how to be loved.

PTSD issues have a lot to do with fundamental derision because of person-to-person lack of trust. How do you trust a society still capable of atrocity? How can the Super Bowl and the Master's go on when people are having limbs blown off in war?

With cognitive and memory processes fraying the tension boundaries within typical normalized   cognitive coherence, coherence is sought elsewhere with escape drugs. The sad thing is how we seem to require a mental vacation induced by drugs. For this reason I'm against drug testing for TTC (Toronto city transit employees). People are unfortunately, at least for a while, enhanced by mental vacations. The alternative is the state sponsored mental vacation--alcohol. Alcohol is a depressant. It kills brain cells.

Alcohol is a mind-eating drug. The correlation between alcoholism and dementia is a profound one that needs to be explored. This is the obvious correlation to pursue. Why does life have to be such a struggle?

The problem for the PTSD sufferer, in a sense, is to marshal the mind so it can re-place itself in a hypocritical human condition without coughing up the soul. Tricky business. The afterlife, just one bullet away, looks appealing by comparison.

If you can no longer construct a coherent narrative you are lost already whether you know it or not. When the only coherent narrative in town is the socially accepted one, the same old same old, one featured and propelled into media purveyance, we are manufactured as fractured selves. We are slaves to an idea someone has about us.

Talking about their experiences helps. ***"Disclosure process itself, then, may be as important as any feedback the client receives from the therapist,*** " (Emotion, Disclosure, & Health, p. 3). Getting it off your chest is a dynamic of age-old recognition. By attributing perspective in finding your voice, towards reconciling your burden, the release process is inherent. It is also inherent in each and every creative act. This means talking about your real concerns helps. Without narrative conveyance art therapy is virtually useless. Unfortunately the Let's Talk conversation has degenerated into recycled soundbites. This can do more damage than good. To trivialize the self is bad medicine.

Talk is cheap. In one of his books, M. Scott Peck describes the type of male who, over the course of a few drinks and conversation, will pull out pictures of his kid at the pub. The point is if he esteemed them as much as he professes, he'd be home with them. He wants to prove he's a regular guy respecting the things a regular guy respects. It's all self-deception under the cover of self-assertion.

To truly talk the talk and listen, one needs to be processing information like a psychiatrist with deep honest concern. To make your deepest emotional concerns into conversation pieces is deeply problematic. So it's tricky business.

These blockages when we can't escape from ourselves result indisputably in mental and physical health problems. Bob Dylan can't write a new song. Why is that? How can something once mastered be never mastered again? If our brains could organize past and present, so that the person going forward is all they ever were, that would be great. The fact is we lose hunks of ourselves along the way. Most assume we should never lose sight of something we could, once upon a time, conjure at will. Creativity is something you plug into, not something in your possession. As Eminem says, the music owns you, you don't own the music.

Flow is flow and no is no. No flow means no go. From the Muses to the Aeolian harp, the divining rod of creativity is inspiration. You have to open your heart if inspiration is going to find a way in.

THE WEEKEND

Singer, Weekend, recently said that to get creative for his last CD he had to get high. The distance between our pedestrian self and our creative self often involves an alleviation of detail. Rock stars are notorious for getting stoned. We are pinned down by who we are. We are hemmed in. We can't think outside the box because the box is internalized. It is categorically us. Without thresholding with expansiveness via creativity we become a foregone conclusion. The mind signs off. The mind signs off more when we are accustomed to being who we are, not the opposite. We become animated corpses. As Fliot says, watching the working class trudge over London Bridge, *I had not thought death had undone so many.*

A painter painting the first painting, a poet writing the first poem, thresholds at the same magnetic electrical threshold as Picasso. The creative adventure mandates the individual frequency. Feeling it, is, feeling it.

You don't need to paint a masterpiece to be thrilled by a creative act. The amazing thing about Picasso was the longevity of the creative process, his unwillingness to be dismissive in a been-there-done-that sense. Once you agree not to be browbeaten by an uneasy left brain you have clear sailing. There will always be turbulence.

Turbulent oceans are often where the best creativity is found. Brushing up against CHAOS can be wonderfully liberating.

One cannot underestimate the role of doubt and of insecurity. Insecurity is empowerment for the true artist as it is for the true believer. Jesus doubted (why hast thou forsaken me?).The Buddha went through the entire catalogue of Gurus and pondered forever without relief. Suffering designs our bewilderment and our need for enlightenment at the same time it condemns us to doubt. Doubt stirs the stew. As 'Saint' Leonard Cohen sings, the broken and the holy Hallelujah are ultimately, somehow paradoxically, the same.

Most art groups are really unenlightened when it comes to pursuing enlightenment. The art group is a shallow reflection of a belief system the members subscribe to and defer to. It's a church congregation where a Van Gogh or a Picasso would be seen as zealots and shown the door. It is distinguished not a whit by its discernment other than the generalized optics of its inbred hierarchical nature and platinum card culture. Churches are this way. Any organization is a church. The high priests of art call the shots. Shallow is as Shallow does.

OUR DAILY BREAD

The community of thought and the expropriation of power over the lives of others, whether it's in the hospitals or the courtrooms, is the result of objectified and at times (too often) exploitative reality. However we justify this to our daily attention spans and self-justification mechanisms, we drift incrementally from primal purpose dispositions. These were once recognized but are now lost in the shuffle of mere on the job training. Performance.

Unbeknown to us, we cross much threshold territory that is then irrevocably gone. Our indifference to gauging what is and isn't intractable, personifies who we are existentially down the road. Some people know what to hold onto. In referring to character expansiveness, this is unquestionably the Jungian goal once liberated from persona entrapment and its concomitant attributes and dictates.

Jung refers to Paul the Apostle and how intelligence and discernment puffs him up. He means this in an expansiveness, positive sense, not a pride sense. What Paul is talking about is character expansiveness that comes from being judicious and open about the 'Christ' doctrine. The nature of the Gospel, beyond its commitment in terms of Faith, Charity, Hope, Belief, etc., involves those organizational needs consistent with growth. The left brain is needed to do the agenda.

I remember a female teacher who characterized sex as 'jumping on each other's bones.' We go out of our way to diminish ourselves.... This grappling image seems representative of so much of the current human catalogue. Like Meursault in the Stranger by Camus, we free-float in identification. Whether shooting an Arab, or signing off on mother and girlfriend or his own soul, he is consummately indifferent. There is no preferred, differentiated, status of being. His mind has never gone there.

Jesus pushed the buttons that ushered him towards his destiny when he overthrew the moneychangers in the church. Roman coins were unclean and not allowed so this was definitively the church establishment, nickel-and-diming the religiously obligated, that Jesus was confronting. It would be the High Priests that nailed him to the cross.

This aggressive exploitation of 'believers' and sacrifices was seen by Jesus as heresy. Many people who buy religion have it so wrong; it kills me as Holden would say. How do you get this stupid, that the left doesn't know what the right does? As I've suggested, the left brain is incapable of the scope required to know the right brain. Right brain is big picture and you don't get any bigger picture than salvation.

In the end, Jesus was not seen as a military threat to the Romans. He was seen as a spiritual threat to the high priest.

SELFIE

He who controls the present gets to fabricate the past.

That's what Orwell shows us: how the information coming in controls the information going out. Past, present and future exist as a picture we download from the commonality of expressions. That picture can be infinitely small, infinitely contrived.

Right wing Evangelists can look at Trump and see a saviour. How does it jive with anything, and I mean anything that Jesus Christ upheld? Show me the scripture where you can compare one iota of Jesus to one iota of D. Trump. Those evangelicals who align with Trump haven't taken a serious look at the Bible for a long time.

The story of the Good Samaritan and the Samaritan woman at the well, demonstrate where Jesus stands on this and the Christian truth.

Wittgenstein pointed out that we don't each have a different interpretation for each and every word. To have infinite arbitrariness in word usage would make communication impossible, so too, only much more so, for interpretations of poetry or music, or belief in God.

The idea that something means only and exclusively what it does according to viewer or reader is ridiculous. The Waste Land, however complex, is easily deduced as an example of the human plight abstracted and existentialized. It's not Mary had a Little Lamb and it's not whatever you think it is. The movement behind the concept that each poem means something entirely different is an assault on the validity of shared and discerned subjective experience. It's odd this is the one place that subjectivity was assigned validity.

That's why tangibility can be confusing, like the sandwiching of facts, aka Orwell's Doublethink. Taken away from one frame of reference and placed in contrariness, it is difficult to comprehend. It's like working beside someone for years only to be shocked with uncertainty when you see them for the first time out of context, in the line-up at the grocery store.

Is not this the sort of fast that pleases me?
To break unjust chains
To undo the thongs of the yoke
And to let the oppressed go free?
Is it not sharing your food with the hungry,
And sheltering the homeless poor;
If you see someone lacking in clothes, to
clothe them...
Isaiah 58:6-7

Beloved, let us love one another
Because love is from God
And whoever loves
Is born of God and knows God
1 John 4:7

How does this match with a guy who says he could shoot someone to death on Fifth Avenue and get away from it? How does this match a guy who wants head bashing and torture? How does it match a man who grabs a woman's 'pussy' like he's grabbing a casino railing? How does his appetite for Nukes match Jesus' love thy neighbour? So, so many church goers are headed straight to hell.

The white right evangelicals are full of haters who cloak and dagger holier-than-thou religion into Sunday School pontification. Common sense is not a reference point of something that exists beyond its manufacturers.

One can only imagine the weeping and wailing and gnashing of teeth that will go on when these hypocrites, swathed in their own ignorance, are rejected by God.

PEOPLE OF THE LIE

The big lie is this: that the socially manipulated image of who we are is the main frame of reference to being who we are.

Never before in the history of humanity has this mainframe been exposed as infested with viruses. This is why lawyers get justice wrong and why educators get education wrong. It is why Christians confuse the most fundamental truths of Christianity. Donald Trump and Jesus are as contradistinctive as contradistinctive gets. Yet the speed of information discombobulates us.

Ben Hogan and Sam Snead, a couple of bigtime golfers, eventually suffered golf dystonia. This is a kind of paralysis that erupts spastically when the tension becomes too much in the locale of hitting a golf ball. The notion behind it involves degeneration in the brain's body map. When you stand over a putt a billion times your body establishes rigidity both in expectancy and form. The need for a robotically accurate stroke has collapsed the portion of body map. Autistics have incomplete body maps. Dementia is similar...we have spent too much time standing on top of an idea of self that is both discontinuous and unaware.

Sometimes the idea of what we are trying to do, trying to accomplish gets in our way.

"...some golfers are excessively process-oriented. They try to control every micro-aspect of every shot, including knowing the status of every blade of grass on the putting green....They constantly ask themselves, what is the angle of my upper hand? What is the angle of my lower hand? Are my feet he right distance apart?...Wait, did my finger drift just then?," (Sandra Blakeslee and Matthew Blakeslee, The Body has a Mind of its Own, p. 74).

APRÈS SKI APRÈS LE DÉLUGE

After taking a couple spills teaching myself how to ski I did some research. Soon my head was full of stuff. I particularly concentrated on my ski edges an inordinate amount. That pre-attention focus robbed me of synthesizing flow and an overall kinetic shape of the experience. The little parallax in my frontal cortex meant I lost the gyroscopic nature. My thinking about my edges reduced skiing to a kind of micro process.

At any rate, as I concentrated on my torso angle, the angle of my knees as well as the pressure on the inside and outside edges, skiing began to confound me. I had to revert to a direct approach; a more kinesthetic, holistic approach. The left brain can get in the way on the golf course, the ski slope or in the game of life. It makes us believe this is the necessary route we have to take to get smarter; that our best step forward is to break it down into steps.

In the section on golf plasticity in the previously quoted book, the alternative method is described as the caveman method; see ball, hit ball. Again, this is a way to dirty the idea of a holistic approach. No one wants to be seen as a caveman on the golf course. After all, they once kicked me off a driving range for wearing a collar-less t-shirt. The left brain wants the controller job. The caveman approach is not barbaric. Rather, it takes into account the contours of self-awareness and the holism of visualization. It is higher degree of difficulty, not lower degree. It means when you step up to the tee your thinking is behind you...it's too late to be of any use. It won't trap you half way through your swing.

SCHOOL DAZE

When I taught English my fellow professionals were hung up on a handful of red-mark items. Syntax, run on sentences, punctuation, etc,. ruled the day. A teacher could look at a paragraph and fault its lack of topic sentence or its misuse of connectives without so much as trying to resolve what the student was trying to get at holistically. Much like Pushkin's education, education breaks learning down into steps. It misses the point of words as conveyors of thought.

The broken narrative is as important as, and more so than, the grammar.

THE LONELINESS OF THE LONG DISTANCE TEACHER

I used several tricks to get around writer's block students perpetually professed to have. One was the writing Olympics where students wrote as many words as they could in twenty-five minutes. They would count the words. Words could be descriptions of a hockey game. Or poetry, or fiction, or journalism, opinion, whatever. I never had one student balk. It's the prescriptiveness that makes students shy with words.

Most teachers are left brain. This is a thought-crime against the mind and against the formatting of mindfulness. Marking grammar and spelling became what teaching English was about. This became a procedural dictate and teachers coming on board got paid to teach according to mechanical writing issues that didn't encourage thought per se. Not only did it not encourage it, it became nonsensical in the minds of one's colleagues to try to get at something behind it all. Teachers hunkered down in the five paragraph deductive essay and developmental thought became increasingly sparse, always victim of a philosophy that demanded accurate phraseology. Insight fell off the charts.

You don't help somebody develop thought flow if you write 'syntax' in red ink in the margin.

This constant dilution of who we are, satisfying ourselves with that which can be objectively critiqued transformed English as a course of study. No longer were there Winstons and Scouts and Hamlets there as cautionary tales......there were piecemeal information tidbits. English as a study of character was broken into another piecemeal data - conveying discipline. The education system which is revealing underperforming students (info released last week) is a headstrong system. You can't bring up topics like analogy or even allegory. The people in charge are no longer familiar with these things.

Unfortunately, the education factory has little left. Education administration is just another brick in the wall, absolutely a Doublethink opposite. The Ministry of Love in 1984 is where torture takes place. Education is where mind torture takes place. It's a place where students jump through the hoops according to rote backdrops. This sets the stage for massive, erroneous chunking, the passing off into a linguistic usage, the left brain's appreciations of hierarchy, the very characterization of circumvented reality. The Brain on Twitter. The twittered brain.

WARREN BUFFET

Billionaire Warren Buffet talks of his circle of competence. This protracted reality involves his business mind, his batting percentage, all in the world of investment portfolio. He says he enjoys thinking about human problems but they don't have easy solutions like business problems. His wife, when alive, was an activist making sure his money went to help the oppressed. Buffet said without his wife he wouldn't have been the man he became, or even the business man he became. I mention this because Warren Buffet is worth many times what Donald Trump is worth but looks at life, in every aspect, oppositely. One of Buffet's charities supports social improvement through the arts. The arts, as I stress, allow people to reclaim themselves. The arts allow us to discover metaphor. Metaphor is a powerful thing in the art of being even more important in the art of sanity.

Warren Buffet's mind is intact, I suggest, because he respected his emotional reality and never thought himself superior to others. Every thinking creature has many considerations to make about life. You only get one chance. There is no run-through, not so much as a dress rehearsal. The unlived life cannot be reincarnated from one's death bed. Everybody, without the utmost care, at some point gets to a point of no return. There is, however, always an epiphany waiting to happen.

Epiphany can be the result of a continuum of insights.

One is pretty much stuck with the rest of their lives. Everything is already on the track. You've left one station; you are headed to the next. But Plasticity holds the promise that the brain can change itself.

Everywhere in the social structuring of events, the business mind has expropriated the human mind. Technology is part and parcel of this and the leadership style of the Trump-stylized CEOs is everywhere apparent. Everyone is equal but some are more equal than others in America. To entertain doubt is important in self-nurturing. To question yourself, to be insecure even, is a strength and a necessary and profound dimension within a dimensional innerness. Everything is balance. You don't make it disappear.

This is why we have to start monitoring the break-up of the aging businessman's mind. The business mind becomes increasingly expedient as time goes on. It has little room for emotional thresholding which often fades completely. It's the terms of endowment trumping terms of endearment. The inherent reality of the business posture refutes inner empowerment across issues involving human complexity and self-scrutiny. For that reason, it is under siege like never before. If we can start focal pointing this issue in the business community we can save people from getting out of touch with themselves.

Donald Trump's mental demise will play out before us over the next four years.

This self-depersonalization at the top is inherent in the application of one's time allocation. Time after time after time, you depersonalize everything. Everything may seem cordial enough but the deals swung on golf courses have a lot to do with time management, hence expediency, not to mention competitive jealousy. Expediency becomes a simple-faced tyrant. A lot of people are willing to sacrifice their emotions which seem so unsettling anyhow, to the notion of getting ahead. It's too commonplace to question.

THE BELLY OF THE BEAST

Technologically know-how is a special know-how, a very depersonalized, defaced know-how. On every street corner, in every house, the velocity gobbles up ancient valuation tendencies. Mental fatigue from stress related to technology is epidemic. The lack of emotional capacity and resourcefulness stands a man in poor stead. The burden of being last year's man becomes a much nuanced thing. The mind sees its life as over before you see it.

We marvel at technology (picture Steve Jobs clicking you through the iPhone seminar on some humungous screen) placed front row centre on the world stage, much as the Trojans marvelled at the Wooden Horse. The Greeks and the Trojans had been at war with each other for years. All the Greek heroes and all the Trojan heroes had been pitted against each other. Many were the displays of courage on both sides (Hector and Achilles) but victory was no closer. Then one day the Greeks had gone home, their ships falling off the horizon, no longer visible. There was dancing in the streets of Troy. The Greeks had left a gift testimonial of the truly epic struggle. It was a monstrous wooden horse. As the revellers partied on, good sense gave way to bad judgement, and the Trojans, in tailgate party mode, managed to bring the magnificent horse inside the city gates. When the partiers were drunk and passed out, a Greek Elites Force descended from the horse's belly. They massacred the inhabitants of Troy and burned it to the ground.

SMART CARS SMART PHONES SMART BOMBS

We marvel at our Smart phones, our Smart TVs and our Smart cars the way the Trojans held the horse in awe. We don't recognize what is in the belly of the beast. What is spilling from the belly of the beast is mental illness. What comes after the dishevelment anxiety is what we have to start sizing up. What can society do to answer the preoccupations that have swept us into a tither? My 17 month old grandniece scrawls through pictures on the iPhone. Great now, but where is it all going?

Where are our minds going? Wherever we are going we are moving too fast to decipher it.

One thing in the belly of the beast is attention deficit caused by the hyper-tense excitation of ramped-up thresholds. Attention span naturally succumbs constantly to what's trending. We are likewise trending away from fundamental features that create mental health. We are bombarding our mental health with an onslaught of information. The break-up of cohesion precedes the breakup of coherence. The speed information comes at us is unprecedented. It uproots us before we can grow roots. We no longer have the emotional resourcefulness to digest navigable realities. The future is up in the air. People don't have time for pure emotions. One's emotions are tangled up with hate and fear and modern anxiety. There is no way to set a course. We are lost together.

Togetherness makes us feel secure. I remember seeing Zorba the Greek decades ago and the Greek men dancing seemed the embodiment of camaraderie and shared-ness. As a third generation Canadian I felt no such culture. My parents were of Irish and English decent. I was a WASP...a White Anglo Saxon Protestant, yet whatever that was to others it seemed insidious and unidentifiable to me. It might be something someone else could see, but I didn't see it.

Years later, watching Little Italy erupt in joy in Toronto after a World Cup Soccer win, I also felt pangs of jealousy. Like seeing the happy Germans with beer steins at the local Octoberfest. I feel less identifiable to culture and to family.

I once lamented this, this soft and fuzzy embrace with overarching tradition. By identifying with tribal associations we confirm historical commitments to attitudes. We are not on our own. Inevitably individuals come along who find ethnic culture limiting. And it is. Religion is often central here. If you don't buy it they'll beat it into you.

Countless books and movies and histories have wrestled with societies that experience open-faced rebellion. Cyclical sociological turbulence is predictable. Our inability to grapple with the male nature is most significantly manifest in War and warfare. In Canada we could hardly be called tribal. Not only is there no Zorba the Greek, we rarely know our neighbours. Few attend or have family reunions. The protracted social reality, however expansive, is far from group-oriented at all.

Wherever you are identity comes at a high price. You identify with things your group identity identifies with. This might entirely misconstrue who you are. Either way it can be problematic.

We hammer away at the front door forgetting the basement.

IN THE DOGMA HOUSE

People believe a dogma about science. Even scientists themselves operate from dogma. The guy who theorized about Dark Energy a long time back was crucified by science, as were innumerable others. CERN recently celebrated the Higgs particle hypothesizer. Earlier they had turned their backs on him.

136

Particularly venomous was the attack on the Continental Drift guy, Alfred Wegener.

It was pure crucifixion.

Einstein's celebrity overshadows the fact there was a group that wanted to murder him. In 1932, when he solicited names for a petition protesting the rise of the Nazi's, he had only one signature besides his own. The Berlin University that had courted him away from Zurich and other world university cities were now throwing Einstein under the bus. Dogma becomes so internalized, so fired and wired with reinforcement steel, those who fall into it can do nothing but go with the grain.

The phenomenon of memory loss is well-revealed in the novel 1984. The methodology by which the senses are corrupted works with twitter-like phraseology and the day to day treadmill function. In the land of third-eye blind information, snippets attain their own scale. They fill the eyeball. In Orwell's 1984, there were phrase cards and automatic novel writers and porn producers. The dictionary was into its tenth edition of removing thousands of words a year, particularly, what they called adjectives and inflators. 'Double plus ungood' works for everything, much like 'likes' on Facebook. We mesmerize ourselves with information's simple-faced continuity mistaking it for a reservoir of re-approachable understandings. But the nature of its admission is discontinuous with structural growth and capacitation exercise. It is a temporary holding cell. The inherent disorientation profiles itself in early onset Alzheimer's. Alzheimer's is referred to as an epidemic. That's because our mental contours are simple pathologies that imprison us. Most people subscribe to an attitude of the mind as a solid construct. A solid state of mind has a profound inconvenience within its heart. It denies plasticity.

You are exposed to what you are exposed to. It can't be otherwise. If what you are exposed to prescriptively shapes your identity and you can't resist its gravitational pull, you are destined to be swallowed by Group Think. As Bare Naked Ladies sing: **Same old conversation same old music same old quicksand.** It was Group Think that overtook Sodom and Gomorrah and a zillion other places. What happens in Vegas stays in Vegas. Evolution looks on you as just another flag-bearer for the status quo. One brain short circuit beset with presuppositions can explode like fireworks, creating areas of synaptic confusion. This happens when you can no longer chunk together your reality as status quo sorted and defined within the intricacies of who you are. Then you have to look for that piece of driftwood in the middle of the ocean - the one you need to cling to.

How our minds work either does good by the brain or forces the brain into unsustainable surmise with crucial and consequential formatting issues. A person simply overlooks themselves while distracted by entertainment features that are dominating their psyche and collective unconscious. Profound consequences in terms of sociology and psychology are currently undeniably omnipresent, stressing out the world. In just 10 years the world has altered dramatically. An upstart like Trump can take over the most powerful country in the world in 18 months.

What this comes down to in terms of mental health has to do with personal choice within the vicissitudes of daily plate operational realities For a time we can choose to resonate in ways favourable to the brain's multifarious modalities. To approach a more well-orchestrated brain we have to dig into the drama of being, and do it on one's own terms. Many are called. Few are chosen. The literal fact of the road less travelled is the absence of travellers. This is disconcerting. It shouldn't be. History, mythology and religion, not to mention neuroscience and psychiatry, spell out the contract. You've got to walk that lonesome valley by yourself. Your plasticity, come hell or high water, is your responsibility.

One has to slap oneself in the face to sharpen up in these times of onslaught. The crowd is herded into a stampede charging over a cliff towards insanity. Is that you want for your OWNSELF? To be part of the crowd? My guess is that it will become clear when the abyss appears closer than anything else noteworthy, even terrorism. Mental breakdown of GROUP THINK is the most threatening thing on the event horizon.

The level of discourse and the content of discourse, in a society plugged into an all-consuming reality is easily controlled. It is a self-serving loop. Get into the server and you addict and control the mind with its key modus operandi formula: SPEED. Everyone's event horizon becomes one event horizon, Kim Kardashian's face and starving children become of one and the same consistency.

SPEED KILLS

Train of thought becomes increasingly difficult as one ages, particularly when the body has issues and you become preoccupied by pain or bodily short comings.

"He had lost the power to act. It struck him that in moments of crises one is never fighting against an external enemy, but always against one's own body. Even now, in spite of the gin, the dull ache in his belly made consecutive thought impossible....Her voice seemed to stick into his brain like jagged splinters of glass," (George Orwell, Nineteen Eighty-Four, p. 85).

Like guinea pigs overtaxed by the environment, we succumb to a networked identity stressed to the max. We've been made to think that the people we became were the ones we wanted to become. We simply run out of mind because our character runs out of ideas about OWNSELF. There isn't enough mind to go around. When the brain turns on itself there is no place to hide. It knows our every trick, our every lame excuse. It's been there and done that with you thinking you knew the way. Now it's giving up on you.

We are trained to miss the big picture; we fail to juggle the events of our lives with any assuredness. The bullshit has smeared politics and entertainment into the same fox hole: an entertainment threshold that drives ratings. There is no truth when one-upmanship rules. There is no discourse within the self and memory falls into pockets no longer frequented in jackets you no longer wear. The self fades from the mind.

 "They remembered a million useless things, a quarrel with a workmate, a hunt for a lost bicycle pump, the expression on a long-dead sister's face, the swirls of dust on a windy morning seventy years ago: but all the relevant facts were outside the range of their vision. They were like the ant, which can see small objects but not large ones….The old man's memory was nothing but a rubbish-heap of details," (George Orwell, Nineteen Eighty-Four, p. 78,77).

It is my conviction that dementia is the consummation of disorganization in the organism's big picture reality. By not recognizing your individual brain needs, you follow the crowd and lose yourself in the details. A life measured out in coffee spoons is not a memorable life. The brain constructs, in terms of dendrite and axon and synapse, are overrun, dishevelled and finally eroded by misguided life-span intentionality.

The more generously you treat consciousness the more generously it responds. Indeed, the love you emanate comes back in kind. To pretend there is little room for growth potentiality is the tight-fisted approach of ignorance.

When it comes to plasticity, it is what it isn't. We can migrate firings and wirings in our brain to heal ourselves and change ourselves for the better.

By limiting consciousness, we deny our brain's creative assumptions regarding rebirth and expansiveness as a life-long target. We deny the inheritance of plasticity that allows us to have a greater role in our mental formatting, the very nature of design always up for grabs but aligned to meaningful principles of discernment. This fluidity of multi-stage awareness means the brain doesn't get trapped in itself. Because of our nature, being an act of becoming that turns into an act of settling in, there is this inherent danger in brain plasticity. You can fire and wire a brain ill-suited to providing the right neuroprotectant climate, a brain repressed in a Jungian sense, a brain incapable of resolving its myths as Joseph Campbell would say. With just the cut and dried cognitive framework there is no haven.

The hand me down reality in our current secular society makes each generation the victim of old notions. The inadequacy of these notions over time is the simple by-product of knowing more of what we need to know more about, and sacrificing our selfhood at the altar of information velocity. This is the age where history, as Orwell put it, is bunk - a collection of alternative facts dancing in step or out of step with personal optic strategies.

"In principle a Party member had no spare time, and was never alone except in bed. It was assumed that when he was not working, eating,

or sleeping he would be taking part in some kid of communal recreation: to do anything that suggested a taste for solitude, even to go for a walk by yourself, was always slightly dangerous. There was a word for it in Newspeak: ownlife, it was called, meaning individualism and eccentricity....It was as though, some huge force were pressing down upon you – something that penetrated inside your skull, battling against your brain, frightening you out of your beliefs, persuading you, almost, to deny the evidence of your senses....If both the past and the external world exist only in the mind, and if the mind itself is controllable – what then?" (George Orwell, Nineteen Eighty-Four, p. 67-69).

The Jungian psychology is so applicable because the neuroscience conclusively shows how psychological complexes can be physicalized and bring the 'identity' down. In the end you are your own spin doctor. Your primordial agenda is for coherence among other things. We need to keep it together in the ways together was defined as a primal direction, a course of action not designed to be subsumed by a current fiction.

How do we operate without benchmarks? In the chapters of our narratives we file things away. We must be careful who we are becoming when we are least becoming to ourselves. Strategies for mental formatting constructs are simply the by-product of daily firing and wiring. It is unavoidable. It happens by default. Plasticity is Saviour or Devil.

Taken for granted, aspects of the individual's existence fail to enervate the necessary existential thresholding to keep it together. The synapse juice and the bodymind's electrolyte fail. You never let up on being who you are. You can't. Then your signal to noise ratio starts to suffer.

DEATH OF A SALESMAN

Willy Loman is the victim of capitalism. He works hard, drives far, can't afford any luxuries, and through it all his reward is a messed-up, alienated family. One in every four kids where I live contemplates suicide. Pretty soon it will be three of four. Our society is flying off the handle. It is becoming signature human effort. Dementia is the result of a pathologically, shallow existence that outfitted the brain with frontal cortex expedience and soul-less, self-mechanized responses. Our only hope for the innumerables is some magic wand cure.

"The Lottery, with its weekly pay-out of enormous prizes, was the one public event to which the proles paid serious attention. It was probable that there were some millions of proles for whom the Lottery was the principle if not the only reason for remaining alive. It was their delight, their folly, their anodyne, their

intellectual stimulant," (George Orwell, Nineteen Eighty-Four, p. 72).

The thing is this: there is an avalanche of mental illness coming our way. It is inevitable. We have lost sight of what and who we are in the scheme of things. Our hate and fear make us anxious about survival. Stimulus across the board is not there. We have located ourselves on a game board where the features are fundamental and basic. There is no finger in the dyke. Society has chosen to eliminate so much of the right brain, of empathy and big-picture awareness, as a matter of course. Chicken Little has been outsourced; the sky is falling. ART and SALVATION.

Salvation is the necessary reality. It is there as part of the grace thing. We can save our brains from dementia by starting a creative journey, by salvaging what is left of us. By accessing neuroplasticity and neurogenesis you can feed your mind with the unquantifiable. Think of all the music generated from the music scale. Think of what 26 letters of the alphabet have added up to in human history. There are creativity wormholes everywhere.

Einstein said*, "I am enough of an artist to draw fully upon my imagination. Imagination is more important than knowledge. Imagination encircles the world."*

Art can take you away from your pathologically contrived identity and establish your own truth, your own absolute relationship with the absolute. You didn't choose your parents.

You are a child of the universe. Art allows you the freedom to see the collective malady and set your course on inner discovery.

In McLuhan terms, we are wired to our electronic universe. For Orwell you take hot and cold and you shorten the distance between them, and you have total control. The population is concocted to live in more and more dimension-less space.

When I was in high school, I brought home my copy of Death of a Salesman, and later, when in university, a copy of the Communist Manifesto. I thought I was potentially liberating my dad from homespun religious ideation. That's not how he took it. He took it that I was out to de-authenticate him and what he stood for. I was enemy. Many religious types see education as enemy.

To enervate your truth is to enervate big-picture coherence. Only that can set you free from the electronic wizardry that is the world. To de-authenticate your life-script determinism is to cleanse the doors of perception. Only then can you see the real picture. You are part of a society snowballing out of control. The options to do anything about anything seem impossibly complex.

CAPTAIN DARWIN

In terms of evolution, and God for that matter, you are a dud. You were trapped by the age-old temptation to go on the road most travelled because everyone you know is there. Like a species representative, you are trapped like a fly on sticky paper to your milieu and within that milieu everything has been added and subtracted for generations preceding the idea of yourself. Evolution looks for the fish that walks on water and you aren't even in the ball park. Your psychology and your emotions and your belief system are part of a cultural package. Everything is a challenge as when the mortal coil is in chronological distance close to the expiration date. We, as a collective, as a civilization, are reaching for the last jar on the shelf.

A society creates sociological forces. Overwhelmingly, humans want to belong because being excluded feels ugly. Humans will deny their own logic and their own senses to go with the crowd. Orwell saw this assembly-line reality and the face of things as incontrovertible.

Most of this hierarchical BS comes to satisfy the male's insatiable need to recognize extrinsic worth above internal contemplation, external measurement (he with the most toys wins) to internal compass. It is therefore, in Jungian terms, a great cover-up. Lurking in the shadows is an inadequate inner self.

The velocity of information displaces us faster than we can think, faster than alternative responses take form. The mind is squeezed into a perspective. Indeed, life is squeezed into a perspective which is precisely why we disembody ourselves with rapid fire depersonalization. To discover that truth and remove you from firmly ensconced plasticity requires self-scrutiny. Empathy is conceptual awareness. It does not make you more social, for that would be endorsement of status quo. It makes you able to read minds, not flawlessly, not without error, but in a way that evolves to a more and more successful platform for self, and hence mutual understanding. Looking for a connection between empathy and social participation is antithetical. Empathy outfits us with the ability to steer around the Fakes, the Slicks, and the Psychopaths. The male mind is impaired by the consequences of pre-emptive realities that pre-determine determinism and foreclose on empathy.

A lot of Evangelicals think they have a right to be stupid. I can only say that God didn't make them stupid, they did it to themselves. The Evangelicals supporting Trump have no clue about the life of Christ and his teachings and parables. For so many Evangelicals, ignorance is their strength. They see education as diluting of belief.

The same thing goes for religious-like art groups. The plasticity has frozen into academic contours and the terrain there has nothing of creativity or originality. They are parasites to old ideas. It is hard to overthrow your own brain when you've fired and wired the mechanisms.

"Baron-Cohen and Belmonte concluded their 2005 review by hoping that it will eventually be possible to identify the way in which 'large numbers of genetic biases and environmental factors converge to affect neural structure and dynamics, and the ways in which such abnormalities at the neural level diverge through activity-dependent development to produce an end state in which empathising abilities are

impaired and systemising abilities are augmented. Such a unified understanding of the psychobiology of autism will offer targets for intervention on many levels' [Baron-Cohen and Belmont, 2005, 119]," (Nikolas Rose and Joelle M. Abi-Rached, Neuro; the New Brain Sciences and the Management of the Mind, p. 149).

Autism is one example of evolution's response to a thematic inclination towards anti-feeling networking. The fact that some are inclined to endorse mirror neurons has to with an innate sense of what they are. Any creative person recognizes such mirroring.

It is my position that this is the reason behind art and catharsis, namely mirroring, finding different angles of composition. We identify with a character to the point of embodying their burden whether it be Antigone, Orestes, Lear or Hamlet. Those of us who exercise our mirroring more often, by probing archetypal structures in our own personal myth, get way more amperage out of the brain response to Hamlet's problems.

That our genetic bearings have bias, as does sociobiological environment, is uncontestable. It used to be thought, not many moons ago, that DNA was a blueprint of life for each individual. This is so far away from the truth now. Plasticity opportunities are profound. The brain we are busy firing and wiring every day is firing and wiring even when you sleep. Stress imprints, and dreams cycle the daily residue. Your brain has a mind of its own.

It sends you out every day to earn it a living. As often as not, you sell it down the river because you are too busy, too distracted by distraction. To have spare time is to be cursed with the guilt of being unproductive.

Creativity can be fleeting. Everybody began to intuit how malleable the mind was and how perception was linked to forbearance through the culture. The boring bourgeoisie was eating its own tail albeit a more plumaged one.

Trying to alter this expectancy would meet with fierce opposition. Stravinsky, Einstein, Cocteau and Picasso offended the sense of decorum that always descends. That's what culture is, a curtain coming down on the future.

Having enlightenment unveiled to one could be, and often was, transforming. A Greek play about the Persians stirred such fury and pathos, the Greeks, out of conscience, tried reconciliation.

The male mind has a plasticity bent out of shape by maleness. Empathy, as my writing supports, is identical with conceptual awareness and the growth of self-awareness. Mess up your self-awareness and bad things happen.

"It could then be suggested that the social brain networks in the medial prefrontal cortex, the prefrontal cortex, the amygdala, and the inferior parietal lobe were the neural systems underlying disorders in theory of mind, emotion perception, and self-agency in such patients (Brunet-Gouet

and Decety, 2006)," (Nikolas Rose and Joelle M. Abi-Rached, Neuro; the New Brain Sciences and the Management of the Mind, p. 149).

We are most messed up by one overriding consideration: we have to live with each other. Self-agency is threatened by modernity. We should know this. Holden Caulfield (Catcher in the Rye), Willy Loman (Death of a Salesman) and Jerry from Zoo Story gave us the head's up. But we don't care for literature anymore.

People are culturally prone to thinking of a silver bullet, a neurobiologically-based intervention. It ain't going to happen. Plasticity distorts the brain's functionality in positive and negative ways. It does this directly due to the organization we gave it. This is your fingerprint. Your neural map. Whether you stay mentally healthy is an outcrop of your big picture pathology. It is a path to darkness or a path to light.

You have to make the call.

Chapter 3 – FULL THROTTLE

THE KID WITH HIS HEAD IN A FOG

I remember, early in my hockey-playing years, a coach doing up my skate laces.

I could never get the tightness right and I could never figure it out. If I went out with the laces pulled too tight, my feet hurt. If I went out with them sloppy-loose, my feet hurt. As a kid, I frequently viewed experience as if across a great distance. Things happened in front of me.

Many times in my life I have retreated into this fog and viewed my life as a comic book strip in my head. People ask me where I was when I heard Princess Di died, or JFK. The event itself eclipsed where I was. Ditto for the deaths of Jim Morrison, Janis Joplin, Jimi Hendricks and Kurt Cobain. I know where I was when news broke about 9/11. I was teaching secondary school. I was on lunch or a spare so I went to Future Shop to scout some cameras. I walked into the presence of two walls of big screens, and on those screens was a plane crashing into a high rise bursting into flame. It was so pure Hollywood, so much the type of movie I considered shallow and immature I couldn't shake that notion. When I returned to class students wanted to discuss what was happening; I reminded them that The War of the Worlds broadcast had, years previously, been mistaken for real. This, I assured them, is a great hoax, a modern twist on an old story.

Being right or being wrong is often contingent on our too-often impenetrable fog. We often overlook things most significant because our stream of consciousness has its own marching orders.

Yesterday I saw a few minutes of Barbara Walter's update on Jim Bakker, disgraced TV evangelist and husband of Tammy Faye. That at 75 years of age he's back to pitching the same pitch shows how a man can be staring straight at hard-to-come-by insight and push it out of the way. One can only see his in-prison one-on-one with God as wasted on a mind too superficial to grapple. Seeing Tammy's cancer-collapsed face was like seeing the original face, a Hallowe'en mask that had collapsed. This is pretty typical in our self-recognition alignment; that the puffed up cosmetic mask collapses so we can take a closer look at the self. Not the store window self, but the forgotten abandoned self behind it. When the head is lost in the fog of its own atmosphere it is pretty much an ostrich with its head in the proverbial sand. I say proverbial because it is a proverb. The stick in the eye covers the same 'meaning'. More of the same territory comes from Greek drama and the power that corrupts Creon making him blind to justice.

Any church organization that allows people like Jim Bakker and Jerry Falwell into church hierarchy is a religion of the devil. Their position is to be informed by the Holy Spirit but by typical attribute endowment. The ordained one is never the Christ-like turn-the-other-cheek guy who most thinks naïve if not childish. The broadsheet agenda of our society and all the pre-sets up and down the line imprison us in erroneous self-manifesting.

What we believe may have no basis. I went out the day the coach tightened my laces thinking I would have a great game. Indeed, the myth in my head to this very day is that had I had comfortable feet I would have excelled at hockey. It is impossible to know whether my laces were done up better or I just assumed that. My performance could have been placebo generated. I expected to pay better so I played better.

Many coaches coach because it fulfills their need to be controllers. Though they are volunteers they are volunteers because of self-ideation.

In the PTL, the organization, like any organization, is dominated by go-getters who go get.

The substantive leader is not compromised by such need. He stands back and lets others get ahead of him in line at lunch or wherever. Educating, policing, lawyering and judging all give way to the same dynamic which is registered and implicated so close to the bone no one questions. It is the way we are, and to most part, the way we will always be. The problem though is mental illness. Information riddles selfhood with uncertainty.

As humans, we gravitate to the wrong things and our neural maps cohabit with syndrome allegiance, containing degrees of capacitation for screening things outside typical territorial range. In the end, the brain gets stuck in its habits and its habits are established societally. We measure ourselves with similar measuring sticks. By this measuring stick a superficial twit like Jim Bakker can rise to the top. Meaningful people with true vision and conversion are shoved aside, elbowed out of the way by the upwardly mobile, those letting nothing stand in their way. In this context, psychological drives are pure animal magnetism, several layerings of genetic frameworks superimposing. Indeed, it's when our puppet charade, as a contingency of where we are, is found out by the brain that it gives up. It knows everything of essence has been concluded.

The early bird gets the worm and the second mouse gets the cheese.

Look before you leap is difficult to construct in real time. One is on a learning curve with technology that makes it one continuous uncontested leap. We are gone before we are here.

The position I'm suggesting is a simple one. Because you have habitually taken your brain for granted your Brain gives up on you. The mind you've put into place for it to operate gets lost in the fog and doesn't cut it. Mental illness is the culmination of mind mismanagement.

A SOCIETY AFRAID TO SHOW ITS TRUE COLOURS

Nails and hair presentation represents a culture of fear. The ugly self needs prettified by the billions spent on cosmetic special effects. In the tumult of our lives we reach for what is being handed to us. In the confusion we simply forget ourselves, get lost in some roundabout, some Hotel California, we can never exit.

With cannabis legalization coming to Canada all the backlash is surfacing like puss from a wound. The psychiatric association that has hooked us on OxyContin, Prozac, Lorazepam and

Percocet has come out hard against the prospect of legalization as have the police. Let's be reminded that in many cities police in charge of drugs seized have turned around and sold those same drugs. Police are also in the low empathy side of the spectrum, making the legalization concept a difficult conjecture. Cannabis can actually cause healing and to be afraid of it is to be afraid of our own shadow.

FAST AND FURIOUS

Alcohol cannabis road test.

I'd do it. I'll smoke while a cop drinks his rum and coke and then we'll both go through the drive test. Cannabis is not intoxication. It is associated with short term memory loss because you let go of chronology. You can, with practice, enter a different time zone where you can space your thoughts out differently.

Doing calculus or attending different things that contradict the 'groove' is not what you want to do when stoned, but writing a poem or song might come easier. The fact that the US Government has a patent on cannabis as a neuroprotectorant should tell you a lot of the regenerative features of cannabis. The fear of cannabis and the lack of fear of rubber-stamped drugs is simply the product of how we have come to think, what we think. The fear of cannabis involves the fear of thought. It involves the left brain giving up to the right brain some big picture relativity.

Innumerable LSD experiments started uniformly with participants painting a shamanic doll. His is too left-brained for

LSD. It takes the energy which should find its random departure points and prescribes.

ANOMALY

Remember the Chrysalids novel by John Wyndham. Spider-Man had a body with long spider-like limbs, while David's friend had six toes. We are now living in a metaphorical Fringes. We don't have spider bodies or abnormal bodies but our minds are mutating into dissociative forms. This is happening at an ever-increasing pace. Mindlessness is epidemic.

This is mind in breakdown mode and sooner or later we have to stop ignoring the signs.

According to a report on an investigation, both the York District Board of Education and the Toronto District Board of Education have systemic discrimination problems and there exists a culture of fear.

So much of where we are going depends on education choices in the next few years. Similar things were found out recently at the Toronto Board where the director was fired over plagiarism. I taught in Peel County and from my experience people were routinely bullied by a superficial, distracted administration. There was not an ounce of interest in education by either Board or School hierarchy. They were micro-managers.

The Ministry of Education was filming one of my wife's classes recently. This should have been done decades ago. I once had over a hundred hours on video of my classes in action and I left teaching 15 years ago after teaching 25 years. A wealth of procedural challenges and success can be enumerated by video. It should be there for teachers wanting to investigate art of teaching versus mythology of methodology. Methodology has gotten us nowhere but the alienated classroom.

On the news today, I saw a spokesperson for a three day conference on the medicinal uses of cannabis. Our society is personified in how this interview was expedited. People in my neck of the woods, without looking into an ounce of the research, condemn by hearsay, as a cultural imperative, the boundaries established by the media and its tokenism in areas that matter. Jodie and Marc Emery are heroes embodying true courage in the face of ignorance. Swimming against the current of bias held fast by those strung out on painkillers and anti-depressants, and an assortment of mind-numbing drugs too numerous to list. All because of this, sports fanatics have problems with larger features of discernment. They prefer to stick to their guns even if it means slitting their own throats. Their plasticity has solidified; they won't budge.

IT'S NOT THE TRUTH TODAY

Death by cop is perhaps something that exists. Few would choose such an ambitious and probably painful end. There is another suicide at work in the collective unconscious. Death by History. The signature apocalypse brought on ourselves by a convoluting reality without securing essence.

Why? The pressure. Pressure is a weird thing. I remember being in a district final for volleyball. The team we faced had gold uniforms. I think they were the Guelph Golden Gaels. They had a pretty professional warm-up. Still, we were undefeated and had no reason to assume we wouldn't be champions. Our coach, Mr. Van Binsbergen, was a serious coach and we were seriously prepared. My first time up to serve got maybe a point. No more than three.

We were losing. I couldn't wait for my turn to serve again. I would turn the tide. I would be hero. I decided on my nothing ball serve as my serve. You have to hit square centre and pop it. It has no shape to it and can be problematic to return. I knew I had to marshal my focus on where to make contact. With all my concentration on hitting the sweet spot on the ball I forgot the trajectory. It went into the net. I had choked.

Where was my head? Of course it was in the fog. Sometimes we think we are attending all the factors but we aren't.

FEELING IT

Coaches kill me who say, 'the one who wants it the most wins.' Who wants it more? Did Ali want it more than Foreman or Fraser? Not on your life.

These coaches have an out when they lose. 'The players didn't want it enough,' plugs the hole of the debate. The rest is superfluous. So even though it makes no sense, people hide behind an idea that alludes to something intangible and personal.

We are under pressure. Our Gestalt is cramped.

Emergence is impossible. Yoga is good because in yoga we discover the million postures in a posture. Your version of the pose is one in a million subject to your peculiar body's way of confronting stress. Your flexibility is wired to your body which improvises posture to answer the daily barrage.

Holden Caulfield wanted to catch kids falling off the cliff into phony adulthood. The contrivance of the modern adult has deprived the species of freedom. Freedom has become part of a larger misconception.

The durability of our lives is very much a thing for question. At the centre is the paradox of the human brain: its need for stability and balance without sacrificing fluidity. When a society educates its young, the shape of the future mind is at stake. The Spartans chose toughness as the criteria to aim for. Sons were raised in a military antagonistic environment, an idea stance that assumes humans are robots. The Greeks saw the advantage of perception about human affairs discounting the superficial early entries. Education of the mind needed well-roundedness because the complex human brain is full of anomalies.

Peggy Guggenheim had a clairvoyant grasp of modern art. Men treated her like crap for not being an artist herself and most disrespected her for being rich. No wonder the poor woman retreated to Venice away from the people who can never satisfy. Peggy's wealthy father went down on the Titanic. Her sister threw her own children off a skyscraper. Peggy also had the unsophisticated oral compulsion to stick her tongue out (maybe a form of Tourette's) while conversing. Gertrude Stein though likewise clairvoyant in things artsy, was totally ignorant of brother Leo's more sincere enlightenment quest. T S Eliot, my favourite poet, once rejected George Orwell. Gaugin undermined Van Gogh's dream of creative synergy. Few artists possess sufficient lateral domain to recognize other art. Dylan seemed to only be the Dylan we iconized on stage. Offstage he seemed an awkward superficial twit, or that's what I'm gathering, reading his biography as I currently am.

Few are they who know creativity as something conceptualized. Few are they who can divert from their own mantra. PTSD, for example, is best represented as an irreversible field. The polarity damage has been exacted and the threshold script reaches into the most poignant areas of the brain.

The brain is a paradox. It is molten plastic, hardening each and every day into irreversible form.

TOWER OF POWER

For years the brain seemed like a clock or a filing cabinet as reviewers characterized its function.

Eventually it was seen as a computer.

For artificial intelligence this is their wet dream, a series of 1's and 01's right through the binary gates of paradise. Reductionism has taken its toll on us, however. Reductionism has undermined our collective self-concept.

 We have belittled our brains to fit the cognitive world. Things are changing dramatically.

"But the growing acceptance of plasticity acted as something of a counterweight to such reductionism. Ideas about plasticity and the openness of brains to environmental influences, from initial evidence about nerve development, through the recognition that synaptic plasticity was a very basis of learning and memory, to evidence about the influence of environment gene expression and the persistence throughout life of the capacity to make new neurons – all this made this neuralmolecular brain seem exquisitely open to its milieu, which changes at this molecular level occurring throughout the course of a human life and thus shaping the growth, organization, and regeneration of neurons and neuronal circuits at time scales from the millisecond to the decade....The plastic brain becomes a site of choice, prudence, and responsibility for each individual," (Nikolas Rose and Joelle M. Abi-Rached, Neuro; the New Brain Sciences and the Management of the Mind, p.52).

You are the centre of your own world. Your cosmos has its orbiting issues. You are a neuromolecular fact that is far more complicated than we thought.

Every day's comings and goings pass through you. The reality of your existence is part mythology, part reality, part internal monologue. The idea of yourself, as well as your hopes and ideals, are implicated as much as they are constructed. You are impinged upon by society. Society measures you and puts you in a box.

"The centre of the world is the axis mundi, the central point is the pole around which all revolves. The central point of the world is the point where stillness and movement are together. Movement is time, but stillness is eternity. Realizing how this moment of your life is actually a moment of eternity, and experiencing the eternal aspect of what you're doing in the temporal experience – this is the mythological experience," (Joseph Campbell, The Power of Myth, p. 89).

Self-help sections of book stores have always had much written about the power of now. Now is complicated because our very threshold for the experience of now is daunted by where we are in our narrative. During busy stretches of narrative we hardly notice the scenery. Now never happens for long stretches. Now is always postponed. Now is propelled as an accession of nows getting us from where we are coming from to where we are going. Now is a necessary evil. Our pre-dispositional stance sucks prime time from now. Now fits different people in different ways.

TAKE IT TO THE NOW

I went through a period of time playing tennis where my mind wasn't accurate enough waiting for the serve. You don't want your mind to be toiling someplace else, going over the tax return at the moment you have to decide you response.

I like slicing under a ball and prefer a low serve. A high bounce means improvise. Calculating what type of serve is coming and where it is going to land can actually be a cognitive process going on when the serve arrives. What I'm getting at here is how the cognitive function actually undermines the kinesthetic response because it's thinking rather than doing.

That's the weird thing - what we notice and what we fail to notice. Norman Doidge, of the Brain that Changes Itself fame, has a newer book on the healing brain. I read it when it came out a few years back now. As I remember, the first story was of a Parkinson's victim whose hiking had kept progression at bay. What seems the case here is a man takes a new and profound interest in his disease-narrative and the narrative enjoying the attention blossoms favourably. Most of Doidge's stories come down to such narrative incentive.

Disposing ourselves differentially to **_now_** can take on a life-long role-playing aspect.

The flow of reality requires subconscious and conscious attending to.

LOVE HURTS

I was reading Reader's Digest at the doctor's office. In the Jan/Feb 2017 issue there is an article on compassion fatigue. Nurses, doctors, even family looking after Alzheimer's parents, or parents of Autistics, all run the risk of emotional burnout. This is hardly surprising. A caretaker's life can be taken over.

Nurses also a face higher risk of Alzheimer's. By becoming a robotic and hence uncaring (emotionally fatigued) CARE worker, one sits on two stools that get further and further apart. On the one hand people are looking to you to help them through a crisis. On the other hand, as you become more detached you are in the midst of your own crisis developing.

God knows you have to expedite your own compassion so you have enough to go around. Needless to say, pathology is waiting to happen. You can fall into habits that include acting out and habitually pronounced affectation. Cops also run the risk by becoming the very people they are supposed to police. Behind a tough exterior this can fester into dementia, depression or PTSD. In our province at the time of my last book 26 cops had suicided in one year (2016). People, who are complacent with their own mind structure, preferring a rigidity construct, pay the price of rigidity. They are often the ones most likely to drift straight into dementia. Their constraint mechanism has warped their time-drive and distorted gratification.

Everyone necessarily is obligated to sustain their own interpretive mechanism. It is that interpretive mechanism that you rely on to keep you afloat and for that matter, to keep **NOW** accessible. This is necessarily somewhat speculative in nature, meaning much of now happens outside our distillation parameters. Now happens to us before we happen to now.

THE TOWER OF THE PAST THROWS SHADOW OVER THE PRESENT

We are, unconsciously and subconsciously, attention-span wrapped up in ourselves many times over. Getting a compass on ourselves is what it is all about whether you are Prince Charles, Lady Gaga or YOU. Anybody can go off the rails and into a frequency that pitches out a point of no return.

Whether Atheists, Agnostics or card-carrying Christians or Muslims, we have to leap over reasonable un-belief to arrive at our belief. Nietzsche said God is dead, that humankind murdered God. We certainly suffocated God to death under mountains of disbelief. Having God out of the way is great. We don't have to bow and pray every time some cataclysmic event or some personal tragedy happens.

We're off the hook—we don't have to save our souls.

More importantly, we can have fun. We can have barbecues and tailgate parties. We can drink what we want, screw who we want and pump ourselves full of drugs without CONSCIENCE. The promo for a new movie coming out talks of a woman newly single again learning how to party and have fun. This is the problem. Some people think partying is the be-all and end-all of existence. They create a mythology around the concept and pump out movies testimonial to the fact. What's missing is following character so-and-so home and checking out their life. Players only love you when you're playing sang Fleetwood Mac. If you are getting, God-forbid serious, they won't touch you with a ten foot pole. To assume that everyone wants a life in the fast lane is juvenile. Fast and furious leads nowhere, least of all to a psychologically comfortable aging. This is Hollywood's version of reality and the Group Think is entirely susceptible to and synonymous with it. Imagine your future plasticity talking to your present plasticity telling you what firing and wiring you could and should do for the sake of future plasticity resource. The movie you are going to remember ten years from now is being shot now.

GOD IS DEAD

...says the headline in the Times, the day the music dies, in Don Maclean's American Pie song. Nietzsche's right of course. They were quoting Nietzsche. Nietzsche's father and grandfather were preachers and Nietzsche had no difficulty seeing the perforations in the message. His family was strict and discipline for him is characteristically different to belief. Man had brass plated a new god, a god forged in the image of MAN.

Our attention span for God has given way to other things. We worship other information. Irrevocably where we constantly fire and wire is where we are enshrined, where our exercise of faith registers as firing and wiring. This is where the cast and the plastic mould move into the substance of you.

An Atheist could be proven wrong. It takes only a tomorrow where God shows up in Times Square demonstrating powers that only God could have. Just as we can't predict a quantum even outside probability parameters, we can't say with absolute certainty that there is no God. A couple mathematicians have God proofs (Godel and Pascal). Atheists are Atheists for one ace-in-the-hole reason. They believe believers invented God as crutch-- a crutch, they could lean on because they are childish and aren't strong enough to stand on their own two feet.

Atheists see themselves as objective and scientific...no crutch needed, no voodoo ghosts sizzling in their fear. Ron Reagan says he isn't burning in hell thank you very much. At the end of the day Atheism is speculative. You believe in it.

I think this commendable that Atheists recognize the hypocrisy in so many droves of Christians. So much religion is just so much honky tonk, (going to sock it to you in the name of the Lord). It does indeed exist because people need a crutch and indeed this is an invented illusion. Looking at cults you cannot believe otherwise. People are desperate to believe in somebody.

People need crutches. Love is a crutch. Drugs are a crutch. Objectivity is a crutch.

People who are afraid of freedom need a hierarchy, a tangible spiritual hierarchy. They are sharing a drink called loneliness but it's better than drinking alone, if you get my drift.

I know sincere believers in Conversations with God (written by Neale Donald Walsch), and believers in angels (who help them find parking spots) and a believer in Ayuhuasca. Formatting for a belief is important for plasticity. You have to determine whether you are being discerning. Are you fooling yourself? Will your crutch prop you up on your death bed?

To say that you know there is for sure no God, means you need to know past present and future. You don't. You may believe with all your heart there is no God but you are no expert of potentiality and possibility. I have as easy a time being convinced that there is no God as to be convinced there is.

The point is, logic only goes so far. In the end the jury is necessarily out.

Both beliefs are crutches. Both offer positives and negatives. The rest is faith. Objectivity cannot get you there. Objectivity is not the nature of the beast.

People who have a personal relationship with God have a track record they rely on. Sometimes God lets them down, sometimes they let God down. They know that God exists because they have felt it with all their heart. From a plasticity point of view it makes sense because it challenges self-perception and conscience in a meaningful way to construct an intangible belief system. It gives plasticity a star to steer by.

It is also good placebo if you believe you are getting help from an outside source. May the force be with you does not, after all, require that you be a Baptist or a Hindu. Einstein's God is the energy behind the universe. That's my God. Having said that, I don't believe there is a religion on Earth that doesn't level some worthwhile image of what God is into our understanding. Jesus works for me because it makes sense. God creates a world and people. Giving out free will, the human race shaped itself in its freedom. The masses fell into an idea of themselves as a concocted by social reality. Jesus came and found out the world is full of unbelievers. They sent him back where he came from. They sent him packing.

KILLING ME SOFTLY

When you make a grave error, most frequently in a domestic situation, you have to second-guess how you made such a mess of it. Why did you invest so much emotion in such and such a person? Shouldn't you have seen the narrative shifting and the end coming?

Without your information processing centre you would be a basket case with only so many nuts and bolts, but without any schemata, and without the glue-ons that hold the pieces together.

You need a central processor converting interface with reality into a consistently evolving you.

As gases in the universe coagulate together forming stars and galaxies, so too, our mental universe occurs.

Directing this process relies on intuition. We fire and wire a thought...say about a new hobby...sailing...and you gather information and experience accordingly. You fire and wire thoughts and activities given any new endeavour you pursue. You learn about it and decide whether it's for you or not. If it's for you, you gather more and more information both theoretical and practical. You are drawn into it. It becomes you.

In your mindscape this is a constellation. You fire and wire many constellations as the idea of you takes shape. There is crisscrossing between your sailing self and the self that is getting home in time before the kids get home. This is your identity. You like bowling, hockey and chess. If sailing becomes a big thing on your calendar then the signals travelling to and within your sailing constellation will be SLICK. You'll expedite the land to water process. It will be familiar. Function will sail through your brain with less and less obstruction as your firing and wiring gravitates into fast and slow orbits. Fast orbits are close to you.

That's fair enough. A consternated constellation is, however, a very different beast, a different kettle of fish.

BREAKING UP IS HARD TO DO

This is why hate can be powerful when a couple who love: split. Your entire metabolism has been in synch with the world of the other. Your entire brain has warped space time to accommodate a person. Your behaviourism is entangled with this person's behaviourism. As Leonard would say, **I brought your groceries in.**

So many firings and wirings have been triggered by this person. The vacancy hole, the absence of presence, in the system, creates alarm and an emotional black hole where the self scrambles to adapt and re-identify itself. There is a big hole to fill when the relationship has been a long, drawn out affair. Where daily patterns used to exist they cannot exist anymore. They are to be erased. The self you used to be is in line to be vaporized. The interpersonal inter-subjective connections in our

172

lives are the most complex. We mess up here and we can mess up our entire life.

When we learn the abc's and the do re mi's and 123's we subsume the structure because of the connectivity lineage. Anyone who tries to clarify their thoughts recognises firsthand the constraints of language. If you don't abide by the inherent rules, you can't communicate. Blake recognised constraint as the categorical breakdown of consciousness, which he called fearful symmetry. We partition the mind. The world could never again be seen as a whole once we start looking through categories to see what we see.

Blake talked about the mind-forged manacles...the way we interface with particularity.... and book-end and bookshelf our minds. If this causality is tangible and functional the right brain process is vague and open-ended. The mind that fears uncertainty tries to nail everything down with a microscope and Bunsen burner.

In science, symmetry and asymmetry, matter and anti-matter, are profound exigencies.

Symmetry is closure. Asymmetry is anti-entropy. Every time you multiply 3 by 3 you will get 9. This consistency seen as high level learning is really low level learning. The brain as sequencer and rational deliberator is really only a small part of the left brain. Compared to conjectural thought, 2 plus 2 is... well... 2 plus 2. Like an application, you constantly use it, and its magic can take over your life. We perpetually allocate our 'NOW' mind to appliance mechanisms. The thing about the brain is this—as you ramp up focal pointing and constellating energies in one area, other areas fall into disuse. These areas are most often representative of intangible information; information that does not break down into 2 plus 2 equals 4. If our education system and our society understood intangibles it wouldn't be so biased in favour of tangibles. As it is, we have turned the Bunsen burner into our beacon, and night has descended accordingly.

MBA - I WANT MY MAPLE

As developing minds strive in their education they see so much significance attached to business administration and science-tech their universe warps in this direction. In a society pathologically inclined to materialism and expedient movement of information, all of reality is inclined to a very prescriptive jump-through-the-hoops methodology. This fills up not only the life of an individual, but the collective life of society as well. Expectations, measurements and gradients establish themselves as rock solid. Monumental, you might say, in terms of what stature certain ideation has. It possesses us in its scale in its achievement formula.

Needless to say, this can be a burden. Willy Loman and Holden Caulfield, not to mention Meursault and an army of other characters, become victims of the status quo. Their status quo necessities burden them and threaten to squish them like a bug.

When society screws you over, it creates desperate backlash. The truth is unequivocal; you have one life and when others force you to live a life that abhors you, you aren't a happy camper.

Autistics, I believe, are the result of collective pathology, a mind formatting dedicated to unobstructed sequencing. What evolution was trying to do, what it was aiming for, is an expedient tangible creature who didn't suffer alienation and existential angst.

They are where they are on the Courtney Spectrum because their inter-subjectivity approaches zero. Asperger's, Psychopathology and Male Extreme Syndrome all gather here. They share absolutely and indisputably the same features if we look at it from an inter-subjectivity point of view. This means their main defining feature is their lack of inter-subjectivity and this makes interpersonal subtlety an un-understandable reality. Conscience is not a feature of their mental make-up. The Sandy Hook shooter had zero-empathy for those little children he massacred. Similarly, the psychopathological business man sees no reason to sympathize with those whose lives he can make or break.

MAXIMUM HEADROOM

"So many things fail to interest us, simply because they don't find in us enough surfaces on which to live, and what we have to do is to increase the number of planes in our mind, so that a much larger number of themes can find a plane in it at the same time," Ortega Y. Gasset, in The Possible Human by Jean Houston, p. 59).

We live in a time of information velocity outstripping our means to calibrate it. Setting up planes of reference in the bevelled mirror's manifest reflections is no small task. The way we organize information in our left brain sequencer is entirely inadequate for sanity sustenance. More and more people are hitting the wall faster and faster. Indeed, bi-polarity, depression, and dementia involve, most noticeably, an inability to inter-personalize in a mentally healthy fashion, particularly their relationship to GROUP THINK. The simple truth involves our failure to value what needs to be valued. By becoming secular materialists we have aborted large districts in the brain. By being obsessed by the tangible, the objective and the up-to-date, we escape freedom. They atrophy, causing circuit failure including overload burnout and wires crossed, tangling the brain in short circuits. When parts of our brain's electrical network go down, the entire grid suffers in ambiguous and psychological ways. We lose parts of the octave. **"There is a Route Consciousness that is not time conditioned….The term 'human' would thus define a certain range in the scale of consciousness – something like an octave in the scale of electromagnetic waves. In that case, the present system implies that it is, in principle, possible for a conscious being to shift his field of consciousness up and down the scale. When such an entity is focused within the human octave it might be agreed to call him human but something other than human when focused in** other octaves," (Franklin Merrell-Wolff, The Philosophy of Consciousness Without an Object, p. 122).

If we respected mirroring in all its complexity, the surfaces superimposed would allow all brain areas to be onside. We wouldn't get trapped in DOUBETHINK. Big picture realities would transcend the petty 'male' mind with its fetish for the objective; the causal. Projected reflective surfaces of all experiential awareness and self-awareness are infinitely complex. This is precisely what the brain needs to furnish the self with big picture superimpositions. Brains are high maintenance. You need to feed your head with the right stuff. That means rolling out the red carpet to all brain areas, not just the highly fashionable left brain agenda. Not just the attention span's parallax in the frontal cortex. The male-oriented brain has forged an idea of self on the anvil of a conviction that is outdated. Either it has no future or we have no future.

"The aphoristic thought is a child of the transcendental and the conceptual. This is the highest form of articulate thought. He who would understand cannot do so with his conceptual powers alone. He must also let the understanding grow up from within him," (Franklin Merrell-Wolff, The Philosophy of Consciousness Without an Object, p. 99).

This is precisely what Jung tells us about religion. If it's not transformative it's not real. Belief is, at its heart, a series of beliefs and non-beliefs experientially relevant to every moment. Far from making this dogma, it is non-prescriptive in nature. Transcendence is the quickening in the hybrid state. Conceptuality involves the perceptual growth of the continuum, the architecture of continued focus undisrupted by attention span entanglement. Understanding grows from within - there is no intellectual equivalent of this process. To think that there is involves misconception entanglement.

Not only do I believe in the profound aspect of study that mirror neurons offer, as an artist I feel I grasp them first hand. A metaphor is a mirror. In his book, A Metaphoric Mind, Joseph Couture establishes an understanding of Native culture in terms of metaphor as vision, a vision of embodiment expecting felt-meaning.

"The agent or subject of this comprehensive, multi-dimensional knowing is the mind. A fully developed Native mind is one that is aware and fully conscious....The 'seeing' mind discovers in self-reflection that it is an ongoing activity that generates what Arthur Diekman calls a process of felt-meaning. In other words, the mind is a living context for thoughts and perceptions, a relational movement. Like all minds, Native mind manifests itself in functions or operations that

are ways of organizing relationships, perceptions, or forms of interconnectedness....Central in this processual mode is the imagination activity. Imagination and Native mind, as I experience it, is the route by which, or the means through which, the spiritual world influences creatively the development of individual and group culture life. In other words, imagination is a capacity, a power that enables, as Rudolf Steiner states, 'the true spiritual world to light up within the individual soul.' In some, traditional Indian knowing is an experience in matter and spirit as inseparable realities, non-dualistically apprehended. Characteristically, because Native thinking is inclusive, it resists simple, abstract objective definition," (R. Couture & V. McGowan, editors, Explorations in Native Knowing in Selected Writings of Joseph Couture, p. 101-103).

If we are to rescue the visions of the THIRD EYE we need to come to appreciate the mirroring that becomes structurally relative to our mind's design. Metaphor, analogy, allegory, parable, poetry - all reflect complexity in the name of inviting more complexity in the name of self-discovery. Metaphor is a way of looking at things, a way that embodies a great deal.

As Frye points out, a slowly transitioning society is more solidly based on its 'mythology,' the things that make it tick. Our fast-transitioning world is anchorless. In our hyperspace, technical world we function in frequency realities that undermine our mentality. Our schools no longer chunk the meaningful respectful of complexity. Rather, they stream information. We twitter our lives away.

LOSING MY RELIGION

The important categories of your existence involve your primordial relativity, your raison d'être, your élan vital. Once you lose this in the smoke and mirrors of an attention span shuffle you are officially out to lunch. That so much can disappear so fast is the remarkable thing about mental breakdown. The élan vital, coined by Henri Bergson in his book, Creative Evolution, describes self-organization in terms of spontaneous morphogenesis of things in an increasingly complex manner. To forgo this mandate is to lose ground with yourself over a life time. A little rain and your memories and who you are go swish in a mudslide.

This shuffling of practical identity with its causality consequence pre-defines every action as a diametric, and hence unavoidable, contextual reality. Symmetry holographs you in your world of forms. You are a character frozen in so many selfies. When the context disappears, all is gone. By losing one's Gestalt one loses NOW. NOW literally never happens. A refusal to acknowledge loss of 'now' is in many ways parallel to losing one's mind.

GESTALT

Gestalt involves the ability to maintain meaningful perceptions in a chaotic world. The important thing involves formatting priorities, and the establishment of a perceptual base, that doesn't simply sway in the wind. These manufactural realities we fall prey to are not any good for a mind, not any mind. Mind becomes a spurious, spastic knee-jerk reaction in an over-taxed environment. As a society losing its reason to believe, we recognize the further drama as ensuing: the failure to believe in life as a valid exercise in energy negotiation. Depression is a recognition of energy depletion, like Wylie the Coyote running into a stone wall. Life from a particular moment on doesn't make sense. The stuff you grab onto is like a drowning man grabbing water.

Coining something like the Courtney Spectrum has manifest benefits. We can quickly, at least in a fluid ambiguous sense, ascertain the inter-subjectivity of the individual, whoever the individual. First of all, in terms of mental structuring, distinguishing a relative positioning away from, or close to, Autism. Distinguishing features in terms of empathy, Theory of Mind, use of analogy and metaphor as communication realities determine the nature of mental risk, and in some cases, therefore, the therapeutic approach. Having said this, narrative-based art therapy is best for anyone. In the art of being sane, nothing has more leverage than intimacy within the self. This is most precious in the creative action. Feeling yourself unfold is a metaphysical reality.

The reality is made more concrete if we see the 90-180 degree curvature. From 90-180, the distinguishing factors are also litmus test indicators of complexity. Human relationships pose for our minds their most complex adventure. Analogy and metaphor extend the range for communication. Art becomes the penultimate inter-subjective possibility.

NEUROGENESIS AND NEURPLASTICITY

With neurogenesis and neuroplasticity we can never ever run out of mind. Cross-multiplying of a hundred billion neuron brains is automatically unfathomable except in respect of archetype. Archetype can tell us where we are on our journey. Are we facing the Cyclopes, the Sirens or the way home? This means that so much can be embodied or chunked in a metaphor as to create a conveyance of awesome information amounts.

Jesus said a man cannot serve two masters. The master of your universe is your most fired and wired circuitry. We masters of multi-tasking serve several masters simultaneously.

This helps any mental health picture to know how and where creativity therapy is most beneficial. If the bowling ball on the bed analogy offered up by Einstein gives us a picture of gravitational pull in space-time, it has conveyed many things at once. This makes it an analogy that allows us to get our heads around something otherwise elusive. Indeed, I know of no other conveyance that simplifies such a hard mental task, of wrapping one's head around such a difficult cosmic apprehension of space-time curvature. It's virtually impossible to think of it in any other way. One can create the barrage of math and add it to

182

verbal description, but such exactitude is worthless if it can't be made palpable to our understanding. The same thing occurs with neuroscience. You have bowling balls in your head requiring complexity arrangements. This warps your gravitational reality in space-time. To pretend this isn't the case is to fool yourself.

PICTURE THIS

This is not simply a case of a picture being worth a thousand words, because the complexity outdistances that. Remember a picture was worth a thousand words a century and a half ago when depiction and photography were beginning. Pictures were very rare things. Now, the download picture stream in its velocity actually discounts the role of picture. A thousand words in a McLuhan world might very likely be many times more poignant than the diarrhea of pictures that daily desecrate our minds. Pictures are cheap. Once upon a time they were expensive.

The mind needs to be versatile. I'm saying mirror neurons inflate the psyche's ability to self-appreciate self and others. Any movement in the spectrum can cause a prismatic shift of untold proportion.

"Mirror neurons are currently a prime suspect in the hunt for the causes of autism. The cardinal features of autism, a congenital brain disorder, are lack of empathy, imitation, language skills, and an internal model of other people's mental

states – in other words, the very functions that mirror neurons specialize in….He (the Autistic) does not connect what it feels like, to be sad, angry, disgusted, or surprised with the minds of the people around him. Their mental aloneness, lack of play, poor eye contact, and disinterest in the animate world are all consistent with a mirror neuron system that is not properly engaged," (Sandra Blakeslee & Mathew Blakeslee, The Body has a Mind of its Own, p. 178).

Mirroring is Gestalt-palpable, it is psycho-kinetic, and creates bevelled edges of metaphor and analogy. The potentiality for big chunk complexity has to do with the type of information and the embodiment nature and subsequent features. Mirror neurons afford the opportunity for big picture absorption.

We need to contour psychology in a way that promotes mental health. To do this puts us in competition with the shapes of forces that rule the air waves. Orchestrating more of the brain's plasticity throughout all brain areas is the most pivotal structural arrangement you can make with sanity. It's the brain's striving for complexity that once thwarted, results in alienation, strife, violence and apocalypse.

The Courtney Spectrum is useful for gauging sanity. Anyone depersonalizing and objectifying themselves moves to the

Autism end of the spectrum. All of society is collectively moving there. The other direction affords an enriching reality in terms of complexity, empathy and multi-expositional perspective gaining. Mirror neurons are the visionary tools we need for Third Eye response, networking within the neural reality, confirming and embracing the complexity of body mind mapping. Complex mental abilities are thwarted by objectivity. What one can grasp by grasping the mind of the other is the most dangerous of human negotiation. A misapprehension of the other is a big mistake.

"Without a doubt it is one of the most important discoveries ever made about the brain. Mirror neurons will do for psychology what DNA did for biology: they will provide a unifying framework and help explain a host of mental abilities that have hitherto remained mysterious and inaccessible to experiments….They allow you to grasp the minds of others, not through conceptual reasoning, but by modelling their actions, intentions, and emotions in the matrix of your own body mandala," (Sandra Blakeslee & Mathew Blakeslee, quoting Ramachandran, The Body has a Mind of its Own, p. 166).

The entire brain systemizes itself into faster and slower realities including how complex emotional realities are juggled. The psyche polarizes great dominions in the brain. It imposes its will on polarity environments that induce favour or disfavour before you know what is happening. This is precisely why we backslide on our more devout considerations.

We are attracted to attention-grabbing reality. This displaces any need to grow deeper, moment to moment. It can create un-navigable distance within the self.

TANGLED UP IN BLUE

Moods sweep over us, changing the climate internally. Our cellular polarities and disposition salute a hierarchy of needs and major movements. These major aspects of brain function are intangible aspects. That's why the new neuroscience has begun to address subconscious and unconscious aspects. If life happened between the goal posts of attention span, we'd be able to make up our minds and follow through. But it's not that easy. Making our minds up to watch less television, go to the gym, and go on a diet are organism-wide issues, subject to past failures and success, book marked into your identity.

ROPE-A-DOPE

Certain speed limits fluctuate according to flow. This is obvious. Some days you have a bounce in your step; other days you metaphorically limp to the sidelines. The ebb and flow of psychological undercurrents become the underpinnings of self-hood. Changing yourself is excruciatingly difficult. Swimming against the current of your moods is no piece of cake. Plasticity turns into thicker and thicker gunk as formats become more unchangeable. When you age within a system of thought, the system of thought speaks for you and passes for you. Your own Ali shuffle or rope-a-dope becomes organized as subconscious realities.

During epiphanies, a reset switch clears the screen of text and subtext. Self, itself, is superseded in one leap by a new brain, a brain that has indeed changed itself. It leaps into a new realm of firing and wiring the way an electron jumps orbits. The old tangle of overpasses, highways and bi-ways disappears in the rear-view mirror. This makes way for a new relativity where valuation carries different weight. Different circumstances that resonate differently are automatically 'known'. You see the 'light' and it lights your pathway forward.

The mind is molten plastic. In a sense it is always in a process of becoming. The more becoming becomes rear-view mirror, the less adaptability the brain has going forward. The more molten, the more it can be stirred, the more it can leap into rebirth. In a sense it is alchemy. A quickening as metamorphosis, flash floods the organism with needles of neutrinos stitching together a different beingness. It couldn't be more comic book or more mythological. The stories of historical lore are ripe for the pickings of just such stories. It is primal. It is transcendental. The more solidified the plastic, the less approachable the brain to anything so extraordinary. The more it prejudges things, the more context implicates itself into capacity organization.

At one end of the spectrum Rainman (Dustin Hoffman movie) can memorize several novels word for word but leverages no emotional connection. At the other end, a sensitive reader can turn Catcher in the Rye into a goldmine of existential wisdom, into a life-changing reality. Catharsis is, I believe, a profound, reunification process. Yesterday, my wife and I saw the movie, Lion. By the end I was a mess of emotions. This feeling avalanche I tried to make physical, to wield it as a strengthening, a healing. When you leave a theatre you are aroused into a state of transport. This internal state is appropriate for psychokinetic levitation. I particularly remember leaving the theatre after seeing Pirandello's Six Characters in Search of an Author. I was stunned. The impact was physical; psychokinetic.

Mirroring takes in what life is, what it can be, where it is going and what might happen. This means applying different thought and evaluation structures and, most importantly, offering more feeling for the plethora of considerations and array of perceptions that put these thoughts in place. Mirror neurons REFLECT the more essential aspects in moving to more complex entity arrangements. This is the golden thread. The self is organized by systematic default wirings unless we recognize potentiality as flow. This is the ancient idea of self as vessel. In Jungian terms, openness reveals our necessary, feminine aspect.

"I was looking at photos of prehistoric archaeological finds the other day and realized that the heart once symbolised female power. It was a procreative, genital symbol: the female version of the phallic symbol. Though trivialized into romance and deprived of its power by centuries of patriarchy, the heart still belongs to us. In a way, history has progressed oddly like a

woman's life: first a time when we were powerful and ourselves, then a long period of patriarchy and forgetting," (Gloria Steinem, The Revolution Within, p. 89).

Women have a profound, primordial sense of what needs to be designated as valuable and irreplaceable. Creativity is identical to feminine acceptance. We open up to the transformative power of self.

If you are the Mamas and the Papas guy who got up in the middle of the night to write down the lyrics for California Dreaming, then you rescued something important for all of us... he could have rolled over for another hour's sleep. You need to be ready for the idiosyncratic NOW. It requires a psychological stance, indulgent of and open for uncertainty. Vision is a combination of mirroring channels alive and frisky, coupled with spontaneous, yet-to-be orchestrated, movement of perpetual discovery.

Metaphorical and allegorical twists are given to mundane situations so we can extract and amplify significance.

The science mind prefers to murder and dissect. It prefers to unpack and drill down. It presumes there is something at the bottom, not at the top. Like physics chasing the core particle only to see it disappear in the Quantum Zoo, hiding behind things that aren't even there.

PAGANINI'S LAST STAND

Einstein wrote poetry, played the violin and did puppet shows. His ability to fathom science came from a capacity to fathom himself. He possessed a creative imagination that needed to become aware of its own mirroring prowess. Einstein said imagination is more important than knowledge. Knowledge builds on knowledge and can only get you the kind of sequential clarity that it can profile. It also gets in the way when you are trying to see over the shoulder in front of you. It gets you further, but only further in terms of where you are coming from, like a ladder extension.

From where you are coming from, your selfhood might well be a short-circuited, circumvented, fired and wired reality-sucking surrogate. Not so good for creative foreplay.

A selfhood, who took over when you were busy making plans, puts your brain on the map ... logic can't get you out of the box. Even when you think you are thinking outside the box, knowledge is invisibly curating your image bank, curtailing your thought scape. Paradigm rules. It's internal. And the internal is looped through the ethereal world of anti-entropy emergence. It is not constipated by the real world and the real world syndrome.

Mirror neurons don't snap together like Legos. They are dissimilar to tangible, concrete reality. It is difficult to make them visible or detectable, particularly to a preordained mind, with zero faith in their meaningfulness. You can't start a fire without a spark is never so true as in a person refusing to see or refusing to hear because of pre-ordained, lock-step perspective. If you are locked in with layers and layers of mis-construance, you'll never have a window of perception to reach the other side. Mozart could play a whole composition in his head at once.

"All this fires my soul…I can survey it, like a fine picture or a beautiful statue, at a glance. Nor do I hear in my imagination the parts successively but I hear them, as it were, all at once. What a delight this is I cannot tell! All this inventing, this producing, takes place in a pleasing lively dream….But why my productions take from my hand that particular form and style that makes them Mozartish, and different from the works of other composers, I do not know," (Mozart, in The Possible Mind, by Jean Houston, p. 161).

I'm suggesting the Courtney Spectrum reveals the number of mirror neurons per cubic centimetre a person has, and how this relates directly to how the brain was formatted. Beyond this, I suggest greater inter-subjectivity enhances insight, establishes conceptual awareness and addresses complexity. All this adds up to sanity.

What it all comes down to is the breakdown of $e=mc^2$: creativity is the source of neurogenesis, and neuroplasticity and conceptual awareness is the door to complexity. Complexity and conceptuality are rooted in empathy. You must feel.

A Montessori child is likely to grow up with inventiveness as opposed to prescriptiveness. If a child has two math professors for parents that child's chance of acquiring Autism is well above the average. Currently, 1 in 79, or some say 1 in 59, children are autistic. A society that bears down on objectivity pushes the child to this part of the spectrum. Materialism and the bottom line is, likewise, a social function that creates pathology at odds with feelings. Society's thematic obsessions move genetics towards future humans - towards a depersonalized, objective, artificial, intelligence society.

BABY YOU CAN DRIVE MY CAR

When I was in university I was told by some that a Bachelor of Arts was useless. A Science degree was what the future was about. Needless to say this filtered down through campuses everywhere. Indeed, today, Arts programs are seriously threatened. They are seen as frills. Recent debates on education privatization points to the incredible depletion of program throughout America's middle and lower income schools. The Arts amplify human inter-subjectivity. Science diminishes inter-subjectivity.

THE FUTURE IS MURDER

People go postal when society antagonizes them and they have no way out. In a sense, according to happiness fulfilment surveys, this is all of us.

The human project has for decades put the money on the wrong horse. Around this misguided ideation we have a built a dysfunctional world.

The way the media skims off information is testimonial to hearing what you want to hear. Those who invest thought structure in the logistics paradigm are having confirmed what they already knew. He who has eyes, let him see.

That the right brain is so much more important than we imagined, astoundingly so, is described with acres of supportive science in the book, The Master and his Emissary, by Iain McGilchrist. Any disputes over left brain-right brain relevance can be found resolved here. The left brain needs logic for its code because, beyond surface literacy, it is out of its element. It can slice and dice, but getting beyond the paradigm is conceptually impossible.

Though I argue rigorously against the positioning of the left brain in commonplace understandings as the executive function, I respect entirely the need for a healthy left brain. This misrepresentation exists because we affiliate left brain function with executive function. My point is this: the left brain functions best when its place is known. It works better, more exactly, when the right brain is happy.

IN SCHOOL

By bearing down on teaching to focal point standardized testing one forces learning into a box.

It is consistent with training principles hung over from Skinnerisms and boot camp-ism.

Standardized testing is okay in the sense of the provincial exams still around when I was in high school. These would ask you to compare a poem and a novel on your reading list. That's not the way they are now. They are more about rote learning and rote teaching kills the mind for any thinking beyond the highly prescriptive. Politicians like it because it seems a starting point. Unfortunately, as a starting point, it can be characterized as starting off on the wrong foot. That system will get continually duller and dumber. It is anti-education fostered by the need for a tangible cow.

Forcing Autistics and others towards patterning squelches any mirror interplay that might occur.

The reason so many scientists and politicians can't see global warming is they can't. The Third Eye is dialed off. They have close to Autism-like mirror neurons. They like the hard facts they can squeeze between their fingers. The scale of their thinking is limited to a horizon of foreground. They like to take things apart and see how they work. That's it. That's all she wrote.

Imagining and conjecturing what can happen in the future, they have no access to hypothetical reality. They are lock-step.

The arts, with metaphor, allegory and analogy, are completely foreign territory to the strictures of the slide-rule brain. Science plods on with the frontal cortex ambulating up to an idea of a self that is fixated on being positionally fixed. It is fixed, fixated on an idea of reality that is biomechanical.

The art schools and the people that populate places of local power are ill-equipped to imagine or recognize anything original. They have categorically fixtured themselves within

Academia. The only real art is practiced by loners like me waiting for a revolution that may never come. Real art is not cognitive. Art education is cognitive.

Plasticity collapses. "Dawkins's Law of the Conservation of Difficulty, states that obscurantism in an academic subject expands to fill the vacuum of its intrinsic simplicity," (Michael Frayn, The Human Touch, p. 8).

SLICKNESS IS A FORM OF CONSTRAINT

We have obscured ourselves by our own proliferance. Generalizations sink into the culture. The people on the inside defensively throw up barriers and hang their hats on a handful of name droppings and a smattering of methods.

Jamaica Kincaid described first seeing a white person. Of course, 'they all look the same' is an early generalization. When the Beatles landed a reporter walked up to John and asked, which one are you? Though the girls knew the difference, I didn't--not early on. They were simply the Beatles.

Early efficiencies in generalizations can become fired and wired, establishing patterns as constraint dogma. Art, on the other hand, is supposed to chunk together one's creativity as a continuum for future resourcefulness. It is the road to insight and liberation from dogma. That's how it is supposed to be.

ASIDE

Unfortunately, arts people have chunked themselves together with piecemeal, fractured pieces, like a Duchamp sculpture; the nude Emperor with no clothes descending staircase beside man standing with cane, orchestrating.

BEETHOVEN'S FIFTH

Habits round us off to the nearest decimal place. This is brain-oriented. Plasticity, once fluid, becomes established as a monument to who you are. Maintaining Gestalt is an omnidirectional quest. One has to re-invigorate by expanding the paradigm not falling prey to the Group Think orthodoxy. One has to find OWNLIFE, despite social attitudes.

Mirror neurons can power transformations because they super-position a human in the most emergent of all superimposition, within the crystalizing forces of conscious and unconscious directives. Big chunks of a person can transform at once. People with super-positioning mirroring see the danger of Donald Trump. He wants to simplify our nature, play checkers with us. It's precisely what Orwell was warning us about.

A MILLION WOMEN CAN'T BE WRONG

The marching women story, far from being something that should be dissed and dismissed, chronicles our last hope for real change. Women and their March should have created a media ripple effect still tangible still culpable.

SNIP

What we don't fire and wire gets pruned away. The male's brain is back to front, firing and wiring from the reptilian brain, uninterrupted, to the cortex. No crisscross referencing exists in the male brain. It likes to get to the point. This is why men like to fight for success. They don't know any better. They have one forward speed, one reverse speed. Both are usually employed at the same time. Often when they have an 'emotional' crash they have difficulty with anything other than a knee-jerk, violent response. Road rage incidents show how a couple of average middle class white men can morph instantaneously into cold-blooded killers.

That we align intelligence to success is entirely contradistinctive to truth valuing. Melania Trump speaks several languages apparently according to media thus qualifying her as intelligent, and even an intellectual. It does involve a style of intelligence quotient, of course, but it's not intellectual which requires conceptual formatting and continuum of insight discretion. She is not an intellectual. Intellectuals don't like to plagiarize.

Knowing languages is one thing, conceptual thinking is quite another. Being able to read See Dick Run, See Spot Jump, in thirty languages gives you no leg up on intelligence. My wife speaks several languages and was on the provincial executive for the Province's Modern Languages organization for years where there are many linguistic savants. Some people have an aptitude for languages. One should not make assumptions that confuse realms of understandings. Language learning involves codification. But, decoding is merely surface literacy; it's not first and foremost idea literacy.

Melania deserves our pity. She lives with a man whose sexual exploits are common knowledge. If he were a carpenter and she were a lady she wouldn't have anything to do with him.

Put a volume of Nietzsche in front of a Trump-male and tell him to expound extemporaneously, and he would not only be at a partial loss, but a complete loss as to interpretive substance. In business administration programs it's all about widgets, not people. Trump's definition of winner and loser is existentially juvenile. Give him and his advisors ten minutes to read TS Eliot and report back, and they will be confounded speechless.

THERE IS MORE THAN ONE WAY TO FLY OFF THE HANDLE

History's second most famous fascist (Hitler being the most famous), Benito Mussolini, said, **"Fascism is a merger of state and corporate power."** Eisenhower warned sixty years ago of the military industrial complex. He called it dangerous. We are now sixty years into military corporatism and the industrialization of the simple man. Evolution has hit a snag. Our minds, complex as they are, are definitively not easy with repressed complexity.

Psychopaths embody character traits which, contextualized, share a space between male extremism and autism.

"One of the most striking peculiarities of psychopaths is that they lack empathy; they are

198

able to shake off as mere tinsel the most universal social obligations...they don't feel deeply, particularly, about anything at all....it's as if they have a learning disability that impairs emotional development," (Kiel and Buckholtz, Inside the Mind of a Psychopath, Scientific American Mind, Sept-Oct. 2010, p. 22).

Few women are psychopaths. Psychopath reality is new ground for women and there is little history. Also, this quote says something hugely important about the psychopath's absorption capacity. Behaviour-wise, they are very constrained and inflexible. They don't respond well to the suggestions of others.

"They also have trouble absorbing abstract ideas, so lectures about personal responsibility are unlikely to penetrate," (as above, Sc. Am. Mind).

In mirroring, we see the key pivotal, self-defining issues becoming intimate with innerness and developmental of ongoing self-awareness. When one's nose is to the grindstone and we are carving out a living, dependent on external reality, we naturally overlook the things of essence we need to beware of. Distracted by distraction, we flounder without knowing it until something knocks us off our mount. Or we are simply there caught up in drama when the apple cart spills and the carpet is pulled out from underneath us. When GROUP THINK fails, thought structures will simply collapse.

By being hunkered down within the event horizon spawned by our personal OVER-EMPHASIZED, table of contents, we miss the boat on redemption. We never wrote those chapters. Redemption means being born again into a new day of self-awareness. We never have time for truth and reconciliation.

In the past, revolutions of consciousness have been what art is all about. Each adventure into post-realism opened up the mind's idea of itself. Official arts circles ironically have art on life-support by restricting the consciousness motifs. Art as a force barely clings to a space in contemporary initiative.

The stress towards academic correlation has destroyed art. No one links creativity, brain plasticity and art. Artists should have more mirror neurons per cubic inch of consciousness than the average bear. They should have more mindfulness, be less petty, less Harper Valley PTA, but they aren't. They are parasites riding into the sunset with the carcass of art.

SINKING LIKE A SUNSET

You've been there at a lake during sunset. You've been touched by your mirrors of your innerness as an expansive freedom sings through your soul.

Vision is sacrificed for indifferent calculus. Keeping our mirror neurons alive is to maintain an eye for innovation, but it is more consequential than that. It is the different world the mind lives in with different ideation, valuation and consequence. It composes a different, counter-variant spatiality. When sunlight turns to twilight, it conjures a feeling of connectiveness. This is your mirror neurons at work. Watching flames in a fire or fish in an aquarium resonate similarly in alpha brain waves.

Super-positioning ourselves above the fray of physics and the impinging learning of diametrical determinism, we can breathe free air. The reason we opted for civilization and not barbarism was why we began to understand and mirror each other. From this we gathered different outlooks on experience and recognized different desires.

Art helps that understanding. Art is not façade. It's not there to pretty-over the ugly truth. This candy-coated life is what art was about in Vincent Van Gogh's uncle's gallery. Vincent could not bring himself to sell this crap. For Vincent, creativity was a human necessity. Creativity involves human amplification

Formatting the mind is strategic to its survival. Without the dimensionality going forward that a fully orchestrated mind counts for, the mind loses itself. It becomes a data-sequencer with no central theme. Theory of Mind, a psychiatric scientific term, makes useful a lot of data joined-at-the-hip. If you know someone else has a mind you also almost immediately know their mind isn't identical to your mind. They have formatted differently; been attracted to different things. The Courtney Spectrum simply puts Theory of Mind on a spectrum describing features. You know how to use metaphor or interpret body language, or not.

The Courtney Spectrum is about establishing spectrally a relationship between all mind formats. Empathy and the nature of inter-subjectivity is the composite human. By seeing things from this spectral vantage point the Courtney spectrum defines, we get a look at precisely those things that move us towards or away from complexity and, most importantly, sanity. This then becomes a useful tool in establishing organization at varying levels and degrees of mindfulness. Out of this can grow therapies.

FAST AND FURIOUS

As information speeds up we lose sight of benchmarks and watermarks. We lose our own mental imprinting ability and our ability to shape reality; we lose our own fingerprints on the things we touched the most. In proving they have minds, people distinguish themselves by firing and wiring differentially. This is why we have to begin to establish understandings about mind formats.

Ga-ga sounds and eye contact begin subliminally acknowledging otherness, though early on it's ambiguous, simply an extension of self-morphing into self and into world. Once one recognizes that other people might look at them the way you look at them, it's a game-changer. Playing up to that fact begins our life journey in competing with some and identifying with others.

If you were Stanley's boy as I was, then you would have had to act like Stanley's boy. Measuring up is measuring to that culture and to your family's disposition. You see the world through the lenses already in place, put there by family, school and culture.

SOCIOLOGY 101: The first principle of sociology as a science is this: Sociological fact consists of a

way of acting, thinking and feeling, external to the individual.

The unavoidability of participation in a social existence predetermines us, at least in range of thought and thinking styles, and parameters inherent to the environment and its culture. Like a fish in an aquarium, your size is determined by the size of the aquarium.

Nietzsche or Spinoza, I forget which, said freedom is being aware of this determinism in our lives. We are handed a life script and there is only a little wiggle room in whom we can become. Being aware of this determinism is a lifelong endeavour. The fix is in against it. Once we relax our grip, any old nemesis can raise its ugly head. The management of one's archetypes, behaviour benchmarks, is integral to your mind's format. Some minds seem formatted for science and math. Others seem formatted for the arts. What are the repercussions of mind stylization? This overarching notion of mind is strategic to saving education. If we don't understand the mind properly we can't possibly understand how to educate it.

Most men prefer to be galvanized within their determinism. To see themselves as emotional creatures is antithetical to the cultural dimension of manliness. Having a heart of stone is commendable. No strings attached. Slam bam thank-you-mam.

MACHINE THINK - I'M IN THE ARMY NOW

In the name of this identity they are willing to trade self-hood. Shaving a man's hair and having him stand naked before a bunch of uniformed soldier personnel is fundamentally reductionist. You never recover from this. This is the Army's professional hazing. It is designed to rebuke you as a person. You think you're somebody - forget it. A soldier has his identity stripped away so he looks, not like an individual, but like a cog in a machine, infinitely replaceable. You are reduced to a specimen. One leg on a goose-stepping centipede.

Certain format features bleed into the ecology of self. Maintaining a dynamic awareness is critical to the ebb and flow of the mind's fortune. Why? The velocity of information exceeds our ability to decipher it. This erodes the ability to field information for the good.

There is a bottom line here. When a human becomes dis-affected the feelings are replaced by one feeling: a feeling of estrangement. Getting over that is a mission. Going to war becomes the biggest estrangement possible.

This is common-place today. By not being able to connect with feeling the self, the identity is set loose in a sea of unrecognizable reality. It's target practice. In the end, the left hand doesn't know what the right hand does. Program discomfiture is unbearable because you no longer have a reason for being who you are. But the estrangement doesn't stop there. You become emotionally alienated from the identity you have bet on implicitly for your whole life, the face in the mirror guy.

Coherent enough means to be integrated throughout the orchestrated self. Parts can't undermine other parts. Atrophy in certain areas backlogs the system. A recent TV documentary on the brain showed a twin getting depressed and this caused a change in her DNA making her DNA different from her sister's DNA. This is rapid response DNA. Autism is a response to the stress on us to enumerate and objectify ourselves. It is generational. Just as this twin's DNA was impacted immediately by depression, Autism is an answer to a stress-request for an emotion-free self generationally navigated genetically.

The mind is molten plastic but it soon fires and wires itself into a comfortable posture. Axons and dendrites constellate synapses according to firing and wiring. Myelin coating assures speed limits and access points for the mind. Myelin insulates the brain from attack of change. Trying to turn your formed mind around can be as difficult as growing a new arm. Losing one's feelings is behind this sense of abandonment and lost-ness. These are characteristics of dementia. In a sense you lose the ability to embrace the self; the self has become something objectified and, hence, disposable.

Losing your foothold in selfhood slips into a more consuming abstraction; abstractions without boundaries. Nothing makes sense. Nothing adds up. Nothing connects with nothing. All mental illnesses are breakdowns in different locations on the spectrum. Most cluster at the border of Autism and the male extreme.

This involves upheaval as mirror neurons are shut down and the imagination disenfranchised. As one approaches DISCONTINUANCE, it becomes, literally, a wrestling match to defragment before fragmentation reaches the point of no return. At this point, it becomes impossible to muster enough plasticity to swim against the flood.

We need to graph is inter-subjectivity. As we approach Autism on the one hand, we have less and less display of inter-subjectivity and Theory of Mind. We have less and less comprehensiveness, meaning we comprehend the big picture less and less. That holds for all of us. The closer you get to Autism, the more the repertoire of available interactions with the world is seriously circumscribed.

TEFLON POTS AND PANS

The ruthless drive of the psychopath's willpower is a mental program fueled by a need to attach extrinsic value to the world. Then he can see it; the phallic skyscraper, the personal jet. A lack of innerness makes the mind hinge on ostensible measurement. If they can't see it they can't feel it.

For all of us the body is always in play. The predicament of the body being attached to our minds is enormous. It has every stick of evidence on you. It knows the falseness and its implicated mortal coil reality.

The obstacle, whether disease or physical issue, brings the event horizon to a crunching, neck-brace moment. Succinctly, as if a curtain coming down, to the hospital bed where you are, the world collapses into your heart beat. You are suddenly not what you were yesterday.

SPOT ON

Metaphor, analogy, allegory, and indeed all the arts, through the creative imagination, are part of this thoroughly differentiated style of mind-formatting. As Kandel (neuroscientist and psychiatrist) points out, mirror neurons are a big part of this, as is empathy. By mirroring, one can superimpose pictures and thought configurations that the linear mind can't grasp. This affords, exponentially, more conceptual range.

Many others are likewise excited about the prospect of mirror neurons and their powers of transmission. We are at a unique point in the history of the human brain.

"Unique human abilities like protolanguage (in which sounds were mapped lip and tongue movements), empathy, theory of mind (attributing thoughts and motives to other people), and the ability to adopt another person's point of view...mirror neurons set the stage for horizontal transmission of culture," (Sandra Blakeslee & Mathew Blakeslee, The Body has a Mind of its Own, p. 171).

The entire nature of education could change.

"It's clear that the end of literary teaching is not simply the admiration of literature; it's

something more like the transfer of imaginative energy of literature to the student," (Northrop Frye, The Educated Imagination, p. 55).

School as conveyor belt in the education factory has to stop. Transferring imaginative energy and culture can amplify us beyond the petty, trigger-happy male.

Theory of Mind is character litmus test, both in acknowledgement of other minds and in terms of ongoing positioning of each of our minds. It is a descriptive of what those minds are composed of and in what manner. Once one sees this, one can apply this mirror to anyone, but of course the more graphic examples representing extremes stand out. Donald Trump is such a case. Xenophobic, misogynist, and narcissistic, he portrays an extreme male with psychopathic leanings. Actions speak louder than words. Trump has no feelings for the marchers, the people stranded in airports, or the people he plans to torture. His lack of empathy and lack of conceptual, big-picture awareness makes him a dangerous man.

Jesus went out of his way to be inclusive to help the downtrodden, the sick and the lame.

Forgive us our trespasses as we forgive the trespasses of others.

Thou preparest a table in the midst of my enemies.

The heart and foundation of Christianity is Love. God is Love. But so strong is the urge to support another white superman like Hitler, these Evangelicals become hypocrites, distorted and discombobulated in their own basic belief system. The point behind militancy in religion is just more Group Think.

"Successful fascism was not about policies but about the strongman, the leader (Il Duce, Der Führer), in whom could be entrusted the fate of the nation. Whatever the problem, he could fix it. Whatever the threat, internal or external, he could vanquish it, and it was unnecessary for him to explain how. This is how fascism comes to America, not with jackboots and salutes (although there have been salutes and a whiff of violence), but with a television huckster, a phony billionaire, a textbook egomaniac 'tapping into' popular resentments and insecurities, and with an entire national political party - out of ambition or blind party loyalty, or simply out of fear - falling into line behind him," (Robert Kagan, Adbusters, October 2016).

The Global Village is the overarching principle. Ignoring the fact is irresponsible. Our children die. Our grandchildren die. We have set the stage for our own destruction. We could have been educated and enlightened. We could have been a contender.

Trump and Hitler come from the same psychopathic mode. On the mental format spectrum they are identical twins. The realm of their initiative is extrinsic to the self. The Art of the Deal is always brokered at someone else's expense.

"Every kind of outward technical progress ought to be balanced in man by an effort at inner conquest, directed towards an ever greater self-mastery. Unhappily, what we still have to ask is whether for an individual who everyday takes more and more advantage of the facilities which technical progress has put at his disposal, such an effort at self-mastery does not become more and more difficult. There is certainly every reason to suppose that it does....I should be tempted to say that the centre of gravity of such a man and his balancing point tend to become external to himself: he projects himself more and more into objects, into the various pieces of apparatus on which he depends for his existence," (Gabriel Marcel, Man Against Mass Society, p. 55).

Muhammed Ali said a man who thinks at 50 the same way he thought at 20 has wasted 30 years. For the psychopath, the same old, same old, pursues him through life's turnstile. Unhampered by emotional baggage, the male animal recognizes he can make it to the carrot sooner without the baggage. Unfortunately, his inner vacuity gives no solace or meaning when the drive dissipates.

Defacing our emotional selves is fertile ground for disenfranchisement of self. Scattered minds are easy prey for the spin doctors always ratcheting up the ante. Too often, one can't get feelings back when they are gone. With behavioural restraints and cultural dogma, emotions dry up over a lifespan. We go out - not with a bang, but a whimper. Most mental and physical illness comes from a dilapidated, emotional self that has cancelled its subscription to its own resurrection.

Our ability to objectify is used against us. We subjugate the body, make it pay for sins of the mind. We blame the leg, the arm or the toothache.

When a rich man like Andrew Carnegie writes a book, professing as he did in, The Gospel of Wealth, that superior wealth implies superior humans, he's automatically accepted as finance guru. Trouble is money can't buy you love. And it can't buy you spiritual at ease-ness, by which I mean mental balance. Greed is a madness.

Luke 16:19 *Now there was a certain rich man, and he was clothed in purple and fine linen.*

The tale of Midas and the beggar, Lazarus, are cautionary tales. Where men accumulate wealth, men decay. In a sense this is like the Affluenza case where the rich kid didn't know right from wrong because his life was so cushy. Wealth insulates one from hardship and the palpable quest in navigating one's feelings. A room with a view is no view at all.

Jesus argued with Pharisees, who believed riches were the reward of righteousness. The Pharisees were all formalism and ritual. Like a lot of Christians, they believe that because they say grace they somehow are endeared by God. Nothing could be further from the truth. The heavy lifting required for atonement and salvation come from the transformative nature of belief.

In the time of Isaiah, (himself a rich nobleman), leading business men in Israel engaged in land-grabbing, as it was called. The oppressed were often evicted by power-wielding landlords.

Lord Byron put it this way in a different era:

There is the moral of all human tales;
But tis the same rehearsal of the past ;
First freedom then glory, and when that fails,
Wealth, Vice, Corruption-Barbarism at last.

NINETY-NINE RED BALLOONS

I'm getting off track, except to say that an inability to appreciate another's suffering is built into modernism. There is constant genetic pressure to evolve in a direction with less emotional 'machinery' with no theory of mind. We are all schooled this way. Our remoteness is built in. Everything is reduced to expedient mechanisms.

For example, the movie Shine exposes the high stress world of pianists competing. That this is antithetical to the nature of music, to the core values of art is never thought about. The movie, Whiplash, is representative of the great American teaching ideology. The very nature of art is in its voice, in its nature, in the feelings brought about are oppositional to such boot camp mentality. Similarly, Canada Grants and Ontario Grants in the Arts have spawned courses on the application method. Can you imagine Van Gogh filling out such bullshit, pages and pages, of jump-through-the-hoops justification? No, nor any self-respecting artist. It's antithetical once again to the very spirit of art. It's bureaucracy designed to reject true art.

I submitted a short film to TVO and its acceptance was acknowledged. Then nothing. I never was told who won or anything. I'm sure they never looked at it.

The arts are lobbied by the usual suspects. The fact that the TVO movie could be longer than 5 minutes also shows the formal tokenism in the system. TV Ontario is out to lunch and the taxpayer picks up the tab.

Every arts organization is hampered by its own affluenza. Creativity is outside the range of operation. These bureaucrats wouldn't know something original if they fell over it.

LIFE IS AN EXERCISE IN FAITH

In the Bible, Doubting Thomas had his faith in Jesus reinforced by feeling Christ's wound. Most of us are not so lucky as to get concrete, direct faith affirmation.

The United Church, I believe, has termed many biblical stories metaphorical. I agree. The understanding conveyed by metaphor has a huge ripple effect. Metaphor is powerful chunking. All history, philosophy and mythology are metaphorical for those who choose to discover life in a manner that synthesizes all-ness.

The picture in our heads of what is going on when we visit the doctor determines self-response mechanisms. Like an organic transplant that hasn't worked, we can reject our bodies simply by objectifying them into blood pressure and annual checkups. Your body is not the vehicle you drive. It is you. Detachment becomes an entropy-prone relationship. We make ourselves believe we are aging. Life itself is a phenomenal organized reality when you stop and think about it. Metaphor and analogy allows us to look at ourselves as if we are characters in a novel.

ANOMIE

Anomie. Anomie stands for social instability or personal unrest resulting from a breakdown of traditional standards and values.

This is us. The turmoil driving the news on our doorsteps each and every day dishevels us, puts us off kilter. Our own minds chew us up and spit us out the other side of experience without grafting things to our essence. Going forward, we have memories only weakly established. More and more from this moment on, less and less people will know their way. Mass confusion is around the corner if we don't come full stop and read the writing on the wall. The media currently, simply through the attention span, have the ability to shrink minds to the size of a dime.

The prevailing winds require enormous tact for an individual to skirt the mass-hypnosis of crowd indoctrination with its mass instinct. For this, one needs imaging power from mirror neurons. The ability to cross-pollinate your own identity with your version of reality determines coherence and sanity.

That's why creativity of any minimal amount excites the organism and liberates.

It's leverage for epiphany which can happen by degrees or as suddenly as a lightning bolt in...Praise the Lord I saw the light. Transport comes directly from empathy and catharsis. Our feelings pull others towards us. The heart reaches out. The breath of dawn is the first day of forever more.

"You have mirror neurons for emotion reading and empathy in two areas folded deep inside your cortex, called the insula and the anterior singulate cortex. When you see a look of disgust on someone's face, mirror neurons in your insula give rise to feelings of disgust in your own body.... When you see pain, you feel pain. When you see someone's upper arm being jabbed with a needle, the same muscle in your arm tenses up and you start breathing faster....This means that

when you empathise with someone's pain, including a stranger's, at some level you actually feel it….These emotional mirror neurons represent both the witnessing and the experience of certain feelings and emotions (women tend to have more active mirror neuron responses and to be more empathetic than men)," (Sandra Blakeslee & Mathew Blakeslee, The Body has a Mind of its Own, p. 177).

The complex nature of our self-hood compartmentalization almost begs the existence of mirroring ability. We need to power up the most powerful aspects of mindfulness: mirroring skills. The biggest chunking that can take place is the embodiment of art of recent movies, such as 'Fences' or 'Loving,' that straps you to the mast and takes you to the heart of the matter. The heart of the matter is the heart of humanity. Art is also ambiguity and paradox and confusion. It is Picasso and Dali, Van Gogh and Modigliani fighting the impossible fight to attain some impossible meaning never before imagined.

Mirroring is an intense operation of superimposed realities - narratives, thought structure, imaginary time-space outcomes. So intense is this mirroring, the outcome is a fluid arrangement of patch-work quilt motifs. Conjectures demand a rigorous intuitive interface. Incongruences are lined up against even bigger congruencies. Mirroring is visionary with a tele-kinetic playbook. Progressive epiphanies follow the potentiation of the mind integrated with its mirror circuitry. The undermining of the value of consciousness in self-preservation motifs was Social-Darwinians on steroids. We fired and wired dog-eat-dog realities, menacing ourselves with competition and fear. In the end, the human died off because they stressed themselves out.

I once photographed my wife, Christina, sitting on Fernando Pesoa's knee. This was downtown Lisbon, 2014, and there's a statue of Fernando in front of a café not far from the José Saramago Museum. Fernando Pesoa authored 'The Book of Disquiet,' a book espousing the benefits of solitude. The manuscript was found in the trunk of a car after his death. In it, he says artists should teach other artists to be alone. It is within such aloneness we get to plumb our depths. Without taking a hike around your own mind, you don't familiarize yourself with yourself. Is it any wonder the mind has had enough of you eventually, that fed up with you procrastination, it throws in the towel?

"This is an absolute necessity for anybody today. You must have a room, or a certain hour or a certain day, where you don't know what was in the newspapers that morning, you don't know who your friends are, you don't know what you owe anybody….this is a place where you can simply experience and bring forth what you are and what you might be. This is the place of creative incubation. At first you may find that

nothing happens here. But if you have a sacred place and use it, something eventually will happen," (Joseph Campbell, The Power of Myth, p. 92).

Premature organization of thoughts from early-onset acquisition and age-appropriate trajectory necessitates conformity with the invincible onslaught of economic and demographic corollaries. Incidents and people create gravitational pull.

Marx said circumstances make men: Men make circumstances. We piece ourselves into orbits of discourse commonplace to our street, our block our town, respective of environment. That there is a huge gravitational pull to make us into artificial intelligence versions of ourselves is undeniable.

Connecting with play is what the arts can be about. Firing up neurogenesis, neuroplasticity and mirror neurons is inherent to art. It's an effort to resonate with spontaneous freedom acts: namely creativity.

SHAKESPEARE'S MIRROR OF LIFE

In novels and poetry and paintings and drama we see bevel edges of ourselves projected into uncommon situations. Hamlet is about to utilize art, namely drama, to watch his uncle's response. His uncle has murdered Hamlet's father and married Hamlet's mother. Hamlet's turmoil is too much for him. What kind of people are these, so shallow they don't respect the gravity of truth, of love, of profound connection? Hamlet is lost in an emotional wilderness. Utilizing drama, Hamlet sees what he made possible to see, something that clarifies his understanding. Like watching Saturday Night Live, it is hard for the impersonated not to squirm.

Without the intersubjective perspective and growth for our subjective natures to evolve, we would be lost in the social conditions that organize and manage the common-denominator human. Like bees in a beehive or ants in an ant colony, we would be patterned. Without firing and wiring your mirroring system, you lose ground with the pure self. The mirroring system provides you with the view. With mirror neurons you can envisage different resonance co-ordinates for your future. Most importantly, it unites body-mind initiatives with new firing and wiring principles and the psycho-kinetic virtue of chunking via catharsis, thereby capacitating new planes of awareness. Cultivating mirroring is a life journey.

Everything gets caught in this historical plasticity determinism.

Life imprints us and contours our brain.

HI HO SILVER

In the Bible, the Elite Army is being chosen. After marching for several hours the weary, thirsty soldiers are taken to the river's edge where they can wash their faces and quench their thirst. Three hundred soldiers keep their weapons near to one hand whilst dipping in the water the other hand. By not letting their defences down they became the chosen ones as this quality was the supposed gauge of battle-ready and appropriate intelligence.

So much relies on criteria. Many elite tests are grafted to an idea that escapes further analysis. The General handing out the Elite Badge chose this one criteria as pivotal. It's hardly infallible. These soldiers might have been too afraid to go whole hog into their thirst. Other soldiers, nimble and stronger, might simply have recognized there was no enemy within miles. Establishing criteria like equating intelligence with financial success is an exercise in futility in the long run. More often than not there is an inverse proportion between criteria design and functionality because of bureaucracy. Our entire criteria for leadership have been shaped by media outlets, Hollywood and comic books.

More and more people are going like lambs to the slaughter through the gates of ignorance. It takes effort to feed your mind analogy and allegory, metaphor and empathy and third-eye, big picture awareness. It is literally swimming against the current.

To develop emotionally and cognitively, we need to individuate innerness big enough to handle the outside world. The world is full of people who think they could read something 'deep' if they had time but that time never comes. Deepness means having a plenitude of planes in a tower of power which is the real brain, the complexity-sensitive 100 billion neuron brain.

Formatting the mind comes down to amplifying certain things and de-amplifying other things, especially built-in tendencies and genetic influence. The stress of our lives forms the contour of imprint in our body-mind.

In a book entitled, **'Neuro the New Brain Sciences,'** concerning the management of the mind, many efforts are made to clarify so much of what is up, architecturally, in the brain. One chapter, personhood in a neurobiological age, typifies different self-concepts across different cultures, each fashioning an idea that most, in whatever the culture, subscribe to.

There are many neural processes across species that bespeak of incredible things. Vast arrays of different cognitive, emotional and volitional states are profiled. Those favouring orthodoxy and dogma are opposed to those favouring imagination and volition. Volition is a threshold of emergence, necessary for neurogenesis. It is the percolation and the stirring of the stew. One writer suggests it's like a record needle in a groove that digs its own oath as it goes around. To rule out neuroplasticity and neurogenesis is a common error amongst science faculties more conscripted to story lines with tangible plot mechanisms and bottom line paradigm mind-blindness.

HEY DRIVER, FOLLOW THAT BUS

My wife and I jumped on a tram in St Petersburg Florida. The bus was a tourist one, beautiful wooden interior, and the driver pointed out the sights as we drove by. We took the same tram the next day, with the same driver who repeated his description of what we were passing in methodical yet animated fashion. Why he didn't use a taped message I have no idea. It was word for word. To do this for several years degenerates the mind's available space. It de-energizes and flat lines activity. Similarly, CNN people, as any news people, have to keep recharging the daily news with slightly different packaging, a voyage of redundancy that many will get lost in.

PARTY FOR THE PEOPLE

I myself once thought I would keep my distance from politics. Now politics is closing in on all of us.

So, I went out to research parties and their processing of candidates. I even thought of running for office. If you want to stuff envelopes and do the dirty work they might have a place for you. The Party has its own candidates groomed by the wealthy in backyard barbecue/cocktail parties. These professional politicians don't understand democracy, they understand politics. Partys shoe-horn into the job the person they want. They make the glass slipper and silver spoon fit that person. There is no democracy. For an average Joe there is no way forward. Try it.

"She had only the dimmest idea of who Goldstein was and what doctrines he was supposed to represent. She had grown up since the revolution and was too young to remember the ideological battles of the fifties and sixties. Such a thing as an independent political movement was outside her imagination….In her opinion the war was not happening. The rocket bombs which fell daily on London were probably fired by the Government of Oceania itself just to keep people frightened," (George Orwell, Nineteen Eighty-Four, p. 125).

We are so tired of politics we resent having to be involved. To vote means that you are buying into the bullshit. To not vote is to forsake the leverage of dreams and accept the truth.

"In the ramifications of Party doctrine she had not the faintest interest. Whenever he began to talk of the principles of Ingsoc, doublethink, the mutability of the past, and the denial of objective reality, and to use Newspeak words, she became bored and confused and said that she never paid any attention to that kind of thing....In a way, the world-view of the Party imposed itself most successfully on people incapable of understanding it. They could be made to accept the most flagrant violations of reality, because they never fully grasped the enormity of what was demanded of them, and were not sufficiently interested in public events to notice what was happening," (George Orwell, Nineteen Eighty-Four, p. 128).

Superimpose 1984 and Huxley's Brave New World, and we have a valid picture of today's world. We have Soma and Surveillance. We have Nero and we have Rome burning. We have 2 plus 2 equalling whatever your boss says it is.

Those with grounding in pre-internet age, or those who have been in too much poverty to buy into self-ingratiating attention-span reducing reality, will most certainly have more mental structure stability. Their chunking and de-chunking are different because of the speed zone information-wise, where they are coming from.

The spiritual and psychological challenge of facing a world in crisis on a daily basis becomes electrically insurmountable when the underpinnings and formatting are increasingly, and most obviously, disingenuous. This is what the boys at the top don't get.

The absolute connection to the absolute necessitates essentiality. Your essence and the essence of being is the interface between species and your identity markers. Your Facebook self is a surrogate sense of self, a graphic marker that heralds the age and, concomitantly, the degeneration and break down of essential process. Once the sense of purpose in all this hits a snag, the applecart full of surrogate items is of no resource to us. It's information that has been passed over for new information.

We are, in this time of crisis, amusing ourselves to death with easiest formatting possible. We let our Apps and our phones, our computers and our TV sets format us. Like an ostrich with its head in the sand, the big picture has disappeared. Mental illness comes from the fact our identities are breaking down. The package of understandings, valuing and interpretation has been ripped from us and trampled on. It looks like opportunity is everywhere, when in truth, opportunity in an old fashioned, freedom-sense, has disappeared from the game.

In the March 6, 2017 issue of Psychology Today, this quote surfaces: **"Children and adolescents with autism have higher level of male sex hormones, which also correlate with the severity of autistic traits,"** **(p. 42).**

As I say, with the Courtney Spectrum, male extremism is a genetic component of Autism. It is a drive towards objectifying the human prototype.

People need to wake up to the euthanasia intravenously at work in a society grown so comfortable in its ideation, that life is simply a redundant follow through. The brain is a garden on various terraces that needs looking after. By watering only the plants in your showcase window you eventually demoralize yourself.

The night has a thousand eyes, sings Bobby Vee. This is how your brain works. A thousand eyes in your subconscious and unconscious realms watch you and mark your performance on the stage of life. You and them have everything in common but some invisible veil separates full-scale apprehension. Every night they take to the bank the day's winnings, the trending stories, the information nuggets. These are our building blocks. They are makeshift commodities by nature. If you are a species representative that got entangled in contemporary society, then you are a child of the age. You live and die by its subscripts. There is no 'you' beyond it. You are consumed by the Minotaur of Modernism. The Labyrinth is your own mind.

By placing yourself outside the circumference of self by subscribing to road most travelled apps, you disconcert the self beyond the means to bring it home. The male organism has cut itself off from its own absolute, existential underpinnings. This is the role model a majority of males live up to. Their fixations are acting out of their unwillingness to evolve.

The biggest mind is a mind super poised in divergent, dispositional realities. From the fixed spot of the turning world, its arch or vista is not positioned in pre-dispositioned discourse. Creativity is the very essence of neurogenesis and neuroplasticity. By creating enough of the time-space continuum to go fishing for the emergent yet-to-be self, we cleanse the windows of perception. Creativity gives us an outreach program to access more archetypal dominion. Creativity gives a message to the brain that all is not over. Things are still going on and new terrain in the neural map is still firing and wiring.

Chapter 4 – <u>TEMPLATE TERRAIN</u>

In our construction of thought templates, the most relevant material is bound up with our personal narrative. Indeed, our psychic structures create and design our cognitive structures. In a sense, we are a force to be reckoned with, and cognitive behaviour is how we do it. When cognitive behaviour dictates the nature of interface, the constrained personality can't reach out beyond the givens. Our personal thought structure has benchmarks of constraint as we comply within the shaded area of the projected expectations of others that tail us throughout our lives. The more plausible speculation has to do with the nature of constraint and anti-constraint. What fences us in and what liberates us. We need a balance that reflects genuine need. Placebo becomes a function of belief deep within the subconscious.

Placebo is anti-constraint expectation motoring through the hosting polarities. It doesn't buy in to the doomsday report. It is, in a sense, non-factual because it transcends facts. Facts are constrained by contractual arrangements with the tangible and the explicit

Art offers the otherworldliness the shaman once explored. Art is there to show a way out.

With my art I feel a need to re-characterize the very nature of painting. My painting should never stop me moving ahead with my subconscious need to explore colour and spatiality. Artists succumb quickly to role-playing and affection within the paradigm. This is very evident in arts organizations who pee on the bushes to keep any outsiders at bay.

That '"The vast wealth of factual learning of the past epoch has left us poor, and out of this sense of impoverishment we are today demanding consciously from art approximately that which primitive people naively demanded. We want art to affect us again...in order to achieve this; we are trying to free ourselves from that rationalization of sight which seems to educated Europeans to be natural sight, and against which one may not transgress without being cast as a complete fool. In order to achieve this, we must force ourselves to that primitive way of seeing, undisturbed by any knowledge or experience, which is the simple secret of the mystical effect of primitive art....The stylistic character of primitive art is not determined by any lack of skill, but by a different conception of artistic purpose, a purpose that rests on a great, elementary foundation of a sort that we, with our well-buffered contemporary approach to life, can hardly conceive," (Rose-Carol Washton Long,

editor and annotator, German expressionism, p. 11-12).

What would you find in the landfill of your mind? A game box from childhood or maybe a car you drove the crap out of at age16? Or if bedsprings could talk, what would they say? And while you're kicking through the layers of objects excavated in your memories what would be there in terms of ideas, vocabulary or intimate moments spent in solitude? What pieces of ideas or thought structures and at what time of your life were certain things important.

He spent a long time watching from his lonely wooden tower/And when he knew for certain only downing men could see him/He said all men will be sailors then until the sea shall free them. (Leonard Cohen)

'Only a drowning man can see him' is an interesting concept. Jungian psychology talks about people in crisis. People seek help when feeling frustrated, when they can't get over feeling stuck. Up until that moment, you go through life without a need to know.

How often have you seen someone on television whose life got levelled by an experience, only to bounce back in a more glorified way than ever previously deemed possible? I wouldn't wish my period of depression on anyone. However, I did learn a lot about priorities. I had misappropriated my priorities.

Sometimes we need a good metaphorical kick in the teeth to make us take notice.

SEVEN TYPES OF AMBIGUITY

Knowing oneself is a term fraught with ambiguity.

A couple months back my vehicle was in the service centre having summer tires changed over to winter tires. When I picked up my vehicle, the steering seemed to be pulling to the right. Normally this means alignment issues or a tire low in air pressure. Because it happened a day after the tire changes I assumed it couldn't be a deflated tire. After all, the tire had to be inflated to be installed. I had reasonable faith it would be inflated correctly.

Yesterday I got my lazy butt beside the car with an air hose in my hand. I found that all my tires were a little down especially the front right. I drove two months (I don't drive much) with my steering pulling me towards the shoulder because I couldn't believe something true even though it was true: my tire was under-inflated.

Self-deception can simply be a matter of putting something off. Then it grows on one, just like accommodating a hip issue we accommodate mental limping.

Once we recognize other minds exist we can characterize how they have been formatted and establish characteristic patterns in the nature of their functioning. We might ask the self to assess another mind to see if it adds or subtracts our ongoing perceptive reality as to how minds differ. If there is something sizable to be learned chances are it will be from another human being that we learn it. That human being may not be alive, but by their 'work' they are just as relevant.

On the one end of the spectrum is the Autistic brain and on the other end, the fully orchestrated intersubjective brain. On the one end is the clinical objective mind and on the other end, the full blown imagination. On the one end you can't guess what someone else is thinking. On the other end you can travel into a Salvador Dali painting that can challenge not only your self-concept but history's self-concept.

The range for inter-subjectivity is a projective range demarcated by mirroring skills. At the zero end of the spectrum, whether we are talking psychopath or simply the extreme male, we are dealing with a highly defined circumference that establishes scope to its scale. The viewpoint is infused with male-oriented criteria.

PRE-CONDITIONS

Jung's term *in potentia* is a good description for the potential of plasticity to make or break the genetic bank. Experience writes our lives with emotional benchmarks. Every over-the-top stressful period indents our genetic expression. It's a case of a life acting as a weather vane and absorbing the ups and downs of life and impressing on the next generation what this generation has learned in the scuffle.

To the extent that societal expectations conjure our will as an idea of ourselves, we march to a drummer who sets the pace for us. To whatever extent that is, our own personal voice gets lost in the din of multitudes.

We think we must conform to the weights and measures as these seemingly standard issue realities.

Because we feel conflicted, but forced to give in, we carry angst.

The fact is, our brains cannot escape what is done to them by the society in which we live and the concomitant social attitudes that envelope us. Your potential is not a pure thing; it is impinged upon by environment and at the end of the day most significantly by the environment of ideas.

Why does little ol' me see this when neuroscientists can't? Neuroscientists, excepting Kandel to an extent, see the subject area through their specialist lens. In a sense, it's like being too heavenly minded to do any earthly good. They are so specialized they see everything from a single perspective. I've done the reading. Dozens of books on the brain have filed their way through my brain. Like a tennis-partner of mine who came to the need-to-know about brain cancer when told he had brain cancer, I came to my need-to-know about the brain, when I sunk into an incontrovertible depression.

I've come to an understanding anyone, who has done the reading, could come to. It's right there. You don't need anything from me in a sense, except this overarching notion of spectrum. By sorting out mind formats, the Courtney Spectrum asserts something never before asserted. Namely, that a great deal of information can be embodied when we provide measure to inter-subjectivity, and discern complexity respective of that.

Corollary to a lack of appreciation for complexity is a precisely descriptive assessment as to the nature of mind degeneracy. Minds becoming more bottom-line and less metaphor –inclined are in danger of positioning their entire mind in a cognitive framework barely bigger than the attention span allows. People don't want to believe this because it doesn't fit their preconceptions. A cognitive framework built on the wrong idea foundation can collapse in no time.

Leaders in the field are too busy to cover the territory I've covered. They probably haven't done more than glance at Eric Kendal's book, the Art of Insight. He's not only a Nobel Prize winning scientist but a psychiatrist as well... hence he is capable of the tangible and intangible overview. There is a land of paradox between the molecular brain and the conceptual brain.

Brain and mind are simultaneous actions differentiated by inductive realms beyond the tangible synaptic reality. From the cubby hole of their accredited specialized interests, scientists see only what their paradigm sees. Kuhn spells out the why for and the wherefore in his book on scientific revolutions. A breakthrough happens, like Relativity or Quantum Physics, and once the new theory points the way toa new paradigm, a rush of scientists chip away at what the theory means. (99% of Science comes down to the chippers). Kuhn shows breakthroughs are from lone wolves getting high on their imaginations, like Albert Einstein.

BLINDED BY THE LIGHT

The brain, as Doidge points out, can change itself. What people don't get is the speed of change. People who are blindfolded can undergo massive plasticity orientation. They can move visual sensory awareness to their touch awareness in five days of being blindfolded. Tons of experiments demonstrate these rapid changes. Imagining doing something creates physical change in the brain virtually equal to the physical activity. Playing the piano or shooting baskets economically fires and wires the same neurology as imagining those things. Just imagining exercise can make a person stronger. When it comes to creativity, the brain can change itself in the most formidable fashion. The slightest threshold can manifest big change.

A distracted mind has difficulty getting in the 'zone' where imaginings register as authentic. You have to believe in your imagination for your imagination to believe in you. Indeed, knowledge is a ball and chain when it comes to breaking through the established criteria of a paradigm.

Einstein also said a couple other pivotal things. Intuition he sees as an abstract projection from his own thoughts, given what he is, at that time, processing in his thinking. Pursuing a problem with intellect, imagination and intuition generates hunches or intuition built on intuitions. Intuition becomes a state of being perpetuated into existence by the interplay of aspects like *feeling* the complex nature of one's own thinking. Intuition is best described as felt-thoughts.

$e = mc^2$

Einstein described being born a human similar to being born into a stampeding herd of buffalo. So powerful is the momentum of history, so weighted is its charge, so fast its pursuit, it's hard to find, let alone register, the sound of your own voice.

Willy Loman, of Death of a Salesman, never knew himself. He was just another soldier of fortune buying into the reality that preceded him. His tragedy is his being normal in every fibre of his being. Poems like the 'Average' or 'The Unknown Citizen' arouse similar portraits. Supertramp's Logical Song and Wordsworth's Immortality Ode show the curvature in the mind towards normality.

All Theatre of the Absurd characters are made of such stuff. Jerry in Zoo Story strikes out at his bourgeois counterpoint before throwing himself on the knife he has planted in Peter's hand. Peter has the perfectly symmetrical life - two daughters, two parakeets, etc. Artists, during the various art revolutions in Paris, often decried the bourgeoisie - why? - because money talks, and the taste for consciousness-raising art is perpetually defaced by popular art, the art that sells.

Why lash out at the bourgeois? They represent status quo.

Vincent Van Gogh only sold one painting in his life time. He had one exhibit (if you call putting your paintings on the wall in a cafeteria an exhibit). Everywhere he went, Vincent met with harshness. Here is a man society has written off as a madman. A madman? - He read all of Shakespeare in English. He read all of

Zola in French. He routinely translated back and forth between Dutch and German. His letters to his brother, Theo, are full of intelligence and self- awareness. His self-portraits demonstrate an incredible psychological range.

"Van Gogh's compulsion to surrender himself unprotected to the world in order to experience its truth, consumed his strength is a short space of years. The way he chose – to create art as an answer to existential anguish and to sacrifice his life when the tension grew unbearable – became a tragically exemplary fate for those artists who sought to unify life and art in the decade that followed," (Lionel Richard, The Concise Encyclopedia of Expressionism, p. 26).

The art world has a comfy arrangement if it has any arrangement with the municipality, town, city, or whatever. The people facilitated often represent themselves on various boards relating to different divisions. They are all afraid for funding and defend their turf like a street gang. For example, a surrealist, married with two small kids, opened a gallery in Guelph, Ontario. He was basically boycotted. Surrealism is a dirty word in art circles because the bourgeois mind is ill-fitted to deal with anything subconscious, anything beyond their trite efforts at thought processing and colour-inside-the-lines art.

THE MAGIC THEATRE

A couple scenes stick with me from reading Hesse's Steppenwolf novel decades ago.

One is, as I remember it, the male central character feels like a wolf of the steppes, a deranged uncivil nature calling him. He's a rebel unwilling to get swallowed by comfort. He arrives from his blizzard trek at the door of his professor. From the door he sees a piano and on the piano a bust of Mozart. The scene confirms in him an idea about domestic, slumbering brains so antithetical to the passion of a Mozart. How did Mozart's wildness end up like this, with an aging Ken and Barbie inside their warm little house? How did Mozart become a domestic pet?

In Beckett's play, Waiting for Godot, the characters are waiting for what they know not. It's like art groups. They are always waiting for something they couldn't possibly recognize if it happened. They tread water in the shallow end. They are more antiseptic than that. This smugness I will come back to. It is not only the undoing of art but the undoing of society. Art Shows are Smug-Fests.

Once normality is under siege, as in 1984, society is easily manipulated in its state of perpetual amber alert. Things go from bad to worse in a flash, and turning things around becomes nigh impossible. In Chicago, the police have conducted themselves as murderers, assaulters, drug pushers, etc., making Chicago into a city where justice is no longer viable in any way shape or form. Cops caused Chicago to be what it is. Yesterday, Chicago made the local news for going six days without a

murder. Culture imprints brains. It's hard to reel in imprinted-
ness.

NATURE VERSUS NURTURE

No matter what our genetics implicate in us, the brain's
plasticity can alter reality forever and ever amen. Not that it's
easily done. But it happens in people every day. Cognitive
therapists can chip away at the same behaviour for months with
little to show for their efforts. However, characters that change
drastically because of character transformation are entirely
different. It's not just one behaviour junction up for change, it is
the entire modality of being. Epiphanies are profound,
transmigrating individuals into all-at-once conversion. You can
make a new man with a new way of doing business. My father's
religious conversion transformed him, and he stayed a convert
till the day he died at 88 years of age.

A best friend in high school in Grade 10 stood 27th in a class of
28. After some protracted effort his father got him into gear and
the last time I saw him he was an orthopedic surgeon in British
Columbia. Your DNA doesn't determine your outcome. The
chance for transformation is out there, if you see it.

Epiphany is one kind of transformation. Respect for
synchronicity opens channels of awareness that amplify human
experience. The ways human experience can become amplified
are multiple.

I remember once he and I had a summer job doing bridge
construction. We came around the corner of the tool shack from
different directions. We were singing the same song line,

Kicking' down the cobble stones and feeling groovy. Since then, in my life, the occurrences of synchronicity have proved innumerable like there is another reality that frequently gets tapped into. True art courts the synchronous moment, plumbs it, finds its source.

It has cemented into my memory how I felt....I was reading quotes (many by Shakespeare) out loud and we were laughing, every aspect cemented into memory with the song somehow part of it. Is it a real memory or a false memory?

THROUGH THE GIFT SHOP

This is where I am with my art, what it means to me.

Everywhere there is expected resistance. I gave an advertised talk in Guelph at a café, and no one came. I saw the guy who works at the art store walk by, probably checking to see if any misguided friend had wandered in. I rented a lecture hall at the university and profiled in the student paper that I wanted art students and neuroscience students to attend. Again, no one came.

Resistance straightjackets 'the scene' into a carefully guarded, choreographed affair. Whatever their idea of pedigree it has nothing to do with creativity or the subconscious. I could go on and on but the bottom line is straightforward enough. True art is dead. We have a comfortable facsimile.

HOLY PLACEBO

Expectations interfere with our reality, for better or for worse. In Australia, an artist took a Parkinson's experimental drug. Warned of potential side effects, he developed, with specificity, those very side effects, only to find out he had been given the placebo. That our minds can create something like this out of thin air shows how conceptions of experience materialize. Think of it - he worried specific side-effects into real physical symptoms.

In an experiment, wine was fed through a straw to Functional MRI testers, and expectation literally altered their taste buds. They tasted according to manipulated expectation. Taste-value depended on whether the wine was said to be more or less expensive. So even deep in the threshold of self, coming to us through the senses, our response mechanisms are geared to eclipse personal physical awareness. We see and taste what we expect to see and taste. The art world has no Third Eye. It grapples and calibrates its grappling like it knows what it is doing when it trends tastes. Nothing could be further from the truth. Our plasticity, our expectations, and most of all, GROUP THINK, rules the day. The side effects and the collateral damage in the minds of potential young artists are pervasive. There is no getting around it.

"The subjective individualism which was its foundation rejects all restrictions and taboos of every kind which might have constrained its initiative. It necessarily increased its means of

expression by favouring, on everybody's behalf, the blossoming of man's most inner originality....They were against the family, teachers, teachers, the army, the emperor, all the henchmen of the established order.

Solidarity, on the other hand, with all humiliated souls, those on the fringe of the system, the congregation of the oppressed, the poor, the prostitutes, the madmen, and the young was advocated....Expressionism is the literature of war and revolution, of the intellectual struggling against the powerful, the revolt of the conscience against blind obedience, the cry of the heart against the thunder of massacres and the silence of the oppressed....Broken lines and forms, disharmonies, dissonances, aggressive colours, and artificial recourse to primitiveness, all these methods were used to provoke calculated emotional shocks in the public," (Lionel Richard, The Concise Encyclopedia of Expressionism, p. 19, 20, 21).

The spectrum of expectation depends on looping adequacies that go soft, turning into domesticated inadequacies. For humans, the social trumps the self-defined self. You've seen those shows on Brain Games where people fail to trust themselves when outnumbered. People follow the group even though they see differently.

Imagine you're sitting in a gallery in Paris or the party room in Musée d'Orsay. Wine is cracked open. Well-dressed people twirl around inside conversations held in mid-air by a smattering of physicists, actors and neuroscientists, all commenting on how elegant, how divine the wine is. You think the wine has a back-bite like Old Sailor. Do you leverage your opinion into the conversation, or do you cower under the wealth of contrary opinion?

Polarities are spectral and characterize the mind. Stress is highly polarizing. Synaptic weightings contagiously adapt in our blood, our nervous energy, to stress regulation because stress is invasive and impacts the entire organism. The breathing and posture, the gait or the immune system, are all worked over. Worry is like imagination turned demon. It can construct our stress-response approach and conjure into being a self-defeating mind structure that becomes embedded in the daily attitudinal modus operandi.

In Jung's psychiatry the shadow needs to be a friend. It represents the denied self. It is what gets lost in the shuffle when we are coming of age, when we are keeping up with the Kardashians.

Gabor Maté's books, Scattered Minds, and, When the Body Says No, and Volk's book, The Body Keeps Score, show the insidious reality of a depersonalized personality. We are creating the poison that inhabits our way of doing business.

NOTHING TO FEAR BUT FEAR ITSELF

Males fire and wire without the left-brain, right-brain crisscross in the corpus callosum seen so much more frequently in women. Just yesterday on a web site supporting a Western Canadian political party appeared the slogan, Feminism is a Cancer. Needless to say, the hostility is directly proportionate to the existent stupidity. The Tom Cruise character in the movie, Magnolia, is of this sort.

I believe this is what is behind the fear…fear of the Jungian shadow that wants desperately to recognize an inner child wanting love. In terms of culture, males have established male-oriented mindsets as a way to the top. Women who succeed often have to mimic this mindset. Of course, we're decades into this and more women have been won over to downsizing their brains just to upsize their wallets. The glass ceiling should be a male metaphor suggesting they can't see through the glass ceiling to higher forms of mental association by way of sensibility and conscience. Males don't stray too far from the tree they jumped from.

Themes in business are so ingrained, the motifs so rigorously upheld, it's difficult to see this as anything other than the necessary prototype. The grid is there co-ordinating its reality. If you are a fish swimming in this aquarium there is only one school of thought. You know that picture of evolution where the fish walks on land and ape turns into man.

Where does it end? Man thrust into a technology that mesmerizes the frontal cortex alluring thought into thinking the wrong thoughts, is an engineering dead-end.

Plasticity is built on a default basis like a house built on the sand. Here today, gone tomorrow.

The business mind is incapable of sustaining subjectivity. Mirror neurons and empathy erode into virtual non-being because of the get-up-and-go overbite of the machine man in a biomechanical, mould world. Un-sustained is the imagination and the soul. In the cramped space of such a scale the human species male has compressed scope beneath sustainable reality thresholds. More and more business men are flying off the handle because the mind turns on the self at some point and the self is found wanting.

In a book lent to me by Dr. George there is a pretty good description of mirror neurons from a book published two decades back. On page 121 it says, **"The observer's brain does not just generate a faint idea of what the other person is doing with their body, but also an echo of their intention in doing it. This allows us to get a glimpse of another individual's plans and thought processes without consciously having to work it out,"** (Rita Carter, The Human Brain).

We have known about mirror neurons since the nineties and yet few people have heard of them.

The role of important information is less and less viable in a flashpoint world. Creativity is a climate of thought. Such synergy was contagious in Vienna in the early 1900's where artists and scientists gravitated to cross-pollinate. Mirror neurons motor the visions of superimposed realities. **"We know that one of the reasons expressionist art appeals to us so strongly is that we have evolved a remarkably large, social brain. It contains extended representation of faces, hands, bodies, and bodily movement, and as a result we are hard wired to unconsciously as well as consciously to respond to exaggerated depictions of these parts of the body and their movement. Moreover, the brain's mirror neuron system, theory-of-mind system, and biological modulators of emotion and empathy endow us with a great capacity for understanding other people's minds and emotions," (Eric Kandel, The Art of Insight, p.500).**

"Solid, empirical evidence suggests that our brains are capable of mirroring the deepest aspects of minds of others – intention is one such aspect – at the fine grained level of a single brain

cell. This is utterly remarkable. Equally remarkable is the effortlessness of this simulation. We do not have to draw complex inferences or run complicated algorithms. Instead, we use mirror neurons," (Marco Iacoboni, Mirroring People, p. 7).

Effortless understanding comes from using mirror neurons.

Studies show that Botox faces unlearn face-to-face communication, meaning a face frozen by Botox no longer has the ability to 'get' a read on the emotions of others; it has been removed. With business types, the motifs they live by are like Empathy Botox. They lose the ability to have emotional expression in their faces and, just as significant, have lost the ability to read emotion in the faces of others.

In the book, Creators on Creating (subtitled, Awakening and Cultivating the Imaginative Mind), the chapter, the Open Mind, begins with these three quotes:

>"If I ever feel I am
>getting to the point
>where I am playing
>it safe, I'll stop.
>That's all I can tell
>you about how I
>plan for the future," (Miles Davis);

"Dare to be naïve," (R. Buckminster Fuller);

"When we think of the creative mind, we think of the generative mind, full of ideas and brilliant new insights. But the creative mind is both full and empty. It is able to create within itself a space for the new to arise. It is a mind that is constantly opening itself to the internal and external world....Some of the most creative minds of all time have allowed themselves to drift into reveries and dream states, into extended meditations during which they courted the irrational, the symbolic, the metaphorical, and the mysterious," (Frank Barron et al, editors, Creators on Creating, p. 56-57).

Novelty is, ironically, considered most important in the work of mathematician and philosopher, Alfred North Whitehead's work, Process and Reality. He says,

"Conceptual experience is primordial fact limited by no actuality which it presupposes. It is therefore infinite, devoid of all negative prehensions. This side of his nature is free,

complete, primordial, eternal actually deficient, and unconscious. ...Viewed as primordial, he is the unlimited conceptual realization of the absolute wealth of potentiality," (Alfred North Whitehead, Griffin and Sherburne, editors, Process and Reality, p. 345).

Here is where it comes together - creativity, plasticity, and self-realization. This clarifies the Jungian shadow in terms of negative dis-ease polarities, presents the infinitude of plasticity, and primordial alignment.

As an artist, I appreciate a recent national geographic magazine that associates creativity with a vagueness of focus. So many suggest it's focus you want. You want your subconscious to focus in fuzzy, metaphysical sense. You want the typical mind supplanted by the atypical mind. You want to open the mind to its most expansive, so associations can leap from nowhere into somewhere. That's a true creative act that opens to possibility rather than circumvents the process with cognitive foreplay. Painting a painting that you design to sell is a cognitive, not a creative, act. Art is not about clarifying focus, about colouring inside the lines, so much as the opposite- clarifying lack of stipulated process, standing aside and letting the imagination have its way. Progressively integrating different ways of seeing, thinking, imagining and presenting becomes a familiar process that can only be entered with the utmost humility. It's not paint by numbers.

Of course we plasticize by default. We shy away from everything except mainstream, broad-road-leads- to-destruction stuff. The herd instinct keeps us saddled up to an idea of ourselves as expedient and commonplace. It's a suitable fit, this contrivance. Darwin lamented not capacitating his mind for happiness by reading poetry and listening to music. Had he done this, his threshold for levity and happiness would not have dried up. Sensibility dies off as we get older, leaving less room for emotional response. A window becomes a sliver of light. A sliver of light becomes a mind that has flown the coop.

Huge expanses of empty parking lots and empty buildings are the places in the brain we vacated. The damage we inflict on ourselves in an attention-span oriented, piecemeal-based reality is happening faster than a life-time of experience can address. That's where we are at, on the brink of Group Think madness.

Daily facilitation amid the demands of daily, autobiographic suppression creates a Society-Mind, indeed, an Autistic Culture. Subjective manipulation dominates atonement subjectivity.

For reference, one can check Matthew B. Crawford's work, World Beyond Your Head: On Becoming an Individual in an Age of Distraction. Other books such as, The Shallows, The Runaway Brain and many others, chronicle the disenfranchisement of self, at least the self we used to consider self. Each has something important to say.

I agree with descriptions of habit performed as self-contingency electronic looping that encourages Autism-like dimensionality. We iron out our velocity of engagement.

Science and capitalism are contributory culprits. Input and output structures and strategies rely on predatorily circumstanced social engagement for money getting.

ANIMAL FARM NOT TO BE CONFUSED WITH ANIMAL HOUSE

In Orwell's Animal Farm, the animals break away from their slave-driver human. They write up commandments assuring equality is enshrined. After Napoleon takes over as dictator, the propaganda minister in the middle of the night changes the commandments. Patriots like Boxer gladly work harder and harder and die in their tracks, never reaching the Promised Land of retirement. In the end, pigs and humans intermingle and Benjamin can't tell which is which. The rules of the game and of human engagement are being re-written.

Art courses have been stripped from schools because science is invincibly practical. Even when I attended university Bachelor of Arts degrees were seen as inferior to a Science degree. Science prescribes de-amplification of the human confluence choosing rather to reduce it to some binary mundane-ness that exists as a snapshot of so little.

The notion that you murder to dissect is why dissection reigns supreme. in Grade 9 science, my timid self had to dissect frog and perch. Methodology and attitude are congruent in the scientific outlook.

Everything is objective, pretend really.

Quantum physics and the collapsing wave mystery dictate the nature of reality as utterly mind-boggling. Likewise, dark energy, dark matter and dark flow are similarly mind-boggling. Our coherence, we so applauded as being total and unassailable, is instead a little piece of inestimable worth as it is part of a larger undetectable reality.

What we knew about the big picture is now a snapshot dissolving in dark energy. We need to set our sights on a new way of appreciating the mystery of self in the mystery of the universe.

Arts allow us to be human to discover ourselves, to make better rules reflective of conceptual understanding. Science blueprints the nature of this discovery after its linear fashion. It knows no better.

Only giants like Einstein and Oppenheimer could see beyond the gravitational pull of the finite repertoire.

Creativity is necessary because it refutes Alzheimer's as pathological. Creativity re-routes the brain. Plasticity keeps it fresh. Constipated neurology is the result of lock-step firing and wiring. The shadow backs up the neurological, psychiatric drain pipes. Misuse of neuroplasticity, and zero use of neurogenesis, clogs the brain's plumbing. Backfiring and short-circuiting criss-cross the abandoned territory. The brain you see in an Alzheimer's victim or a cocaine addict is a frazzled brain most easily observed as an electrical burn-out. Overwhelmed regulators. Circuit breakers that weren't up for the job.

A super important, recent discovery profiles how people with similar amounts of brain plaque are dissimilar in their resource neurology. Remember, brain plaque is the formation that seems noticeably present in Alzheimer's victims.

Though they have the same levels of plaque, the ones with a side-bar of neurons, a firing-wiring reservoir, don't have dementia. This resource configures, I suspect, from neuroplasticity learned throughout the life-journey. Even though parts of their brain are floating off into discontinuity, new loops of neurons are coming into the program. Neurogenesis is the most likely source, personified as explorative mindset and hence, newness unfolding.

Dopamine-Serotonin equations depend on a multiplicity of factors. They depend mostly on autobiographical incentive towards enlargement or containment. Hiding behind affectation means falling prey to our own contrivance. We contain our own enlargement. As TS Eliot says, 'preparing a face to meet a face' and 'measuring out our life in coffee spoons' dogs the idea of selfhood.

To see what is wrong you have to transcend the milieu. To court the continuously evolving self seems ridiculous given the finiteness of reality. Think of popular songs. The songs from the 1920's, 1930's, 1980's and 2017 enjoy a multiplicity of styles. One would have thought that with 26 letters in the alphabet and a handful of notes across a handful of scales that we would have exhausted the song bank long ago. Not So.

Creativity is infinite. Creativity is a wormhole in the mind.

With the brain every moment is being reconciled...every day is a day of judgement. Either you are culminating in one direction or you are culminating in another. Either you are more intimate with yourself or you are more estranged.

Finding our core self in a lobotomized world is the strategy of truth. Growth is required. Remember, Muhammed Ali said a man who thinks the same way at 50 as he did at 20 has wasted 30 years of his life. This goes double and triple for 50-70 age brackets. Why? You tend to resent yourself more in this age bracket. You have more to reconcile.

One has to realize you can simultaneously amass a fortune and waste your life.

I'd be amiss not to mention the Cerebral Symphony by third generation neurobiologist, William H. Calvin, a book I didn't discover until my first book was written. And now I've misplaced it, and can't directly reference it as much as I would like to.

It was a great book that mapped the neuron and the weightings of its attachment constructs, mediated to a self-regulation rate. This weighting attaches significance gradated according to autobiographical incentive and concomitant polarization. What is great about Calvin's book is his notion about narrative. He beautifully incorporates events around him at Cape Cod.

Narrative is crucial. My wife Christina has a book out, titled, Narrative Insights: The Art of Teaching and Learning. Every day we live out our own reality, a reality hard to describe to another person. Essential to our plans are the plans of others. Narrative secures or undermines the brain.

I have a grand-nephew who is one of a group of students selected to the Nano research program at the University of Waterloo. He has already published a paper in analytical chemistry. It deals with agency testing and a new method that is faster and less expensive.

I think microchannel research, though offering a wealth of variables and insights, is not the place where Alzheimer's can be addressed. It would constitute looking for a needle in the wrong haystack to think pathology arises in chemical reality, or that a silver bullet, plaque-eater candidate solution, will come forward. It's time to get real.

"Mental disorders are problems of persons, not of brains. Mental disorders are not problems of brains in labs, but of human beings in time, space, culture and history....Diagnosis is a practice governed by its own rules,"(Nikolas Rose and Joelle M. Abi-Rached, Neuro, p.140).

We feature ourselves in our daily thoughts. Sometimes we sink so low as to question our right to be here. To think our thought-scape is not the reason behind our brain's breakdown is not only preposterous but reveals deeply entrenched denial. We want a chemical silver bullet for cancer and for Alzheimer's and PTSD. The thing is, we need to rethink ourselves. Humanity and civilization in particular are at a crossroads. You have to know when to hold 'em and when to fold 'em.

LUCY IN THE SKY WITH DIAMONDS

I'm mentioning LSD because it may be the thing needed for mass therapy if it comes to that. It may seem the unlikeliest of saviour drugs. The point is it has the ability to allow an individual to sort out self-hood and add mirroring dimensionality to an otherwise flat lining reality. LSD is very Jungian in its ability to gain complete ego release. There is an LSD documentary occasionally shown on TV. Soldiers are standing around laughing their fool heads off. They are on LSD. They are totally non-aggressive. LSD and cannabis have been characterised negatively and this has dirtied our attitude towards them for many they are irrevocably affiliated with criminality and/or craziness.

Literally thousands of studies on LSD, and its epiphany-inducing leverage, have been amassed. It seems criminal that there isn't more access to research. It has been proven to correct alcoholism, bi-polarity, depression and PTSD. People think Ayahuasca is powerful in recognizing and resurrecting the mind, but it pales by comparison to LSD, as I made clear to Gabor Maté at a lecture at University of Toronto a couple years back. He was lecturing on Ayahuasca. In the compilation, Hallucinogens, edited by Charles S. Grob, the experiences of world famous nutritionist, Adelle Davis, is notable and representative of the sort of epiphany that can be dished up. In her book, Exploring Inner Space, she reflects on that experience and a year before her death says, " If I had an Aladdin's lamp, I would make a wish that all persons who desired to take LSD, could do so and that I might be given it approximately twice a year," (Charles S. Grob, Hallucinogens, p. 63).

255

Movie stars, divinity students, and many of the who's who in America, including JFK, have taken LSD.

LSD blows the mind-- sending up old structures as so much smoke signal--- a puff of the firmament lost in the infinite. It is, however, very subconscious, unconscious sensitive, and if you are found, as Johnny Cash sang, 'weighed in the balance and found wanting,' you will be in trouble. This is why the CIA experimented with it as a truth serum...LSD can catch you midstride in playing yourself false. The environment launch is everything. This is why people had bad trips. Many used LSD and any other drug they could get their hands on. Most everyone moved on to the hard, addictive, stuff like cocaine, heroin or MDMA. When supplies dried up they sat down beside the TV with a bottle of Crown Royal.

The Americans have created a Frankenstein that rules the world, policing everybody's drug policies. This is because the American worships the golden calf with a John Wayne mentality. And John Waynes are terrified by the word consciousness. They think it is a word the communists invented.

What the brain comes down to is alignment of agency. Agency is a complex thing with multiple dimensions and modalities. It's not intention which may well be contrived, it's bigger. Intention comes from measuring up. Agency is primal.

Confuse the alignment, and the brain polarizes in any number of ways. Because we exploit ourselves to get ahead, we make expedient choices in our life narratives, thinking we can always come back to the autobiographical self. This shrinks the brain. It withdraws from firing and wiring in essential fluid arrangement designated areas: areas of irrefutable essence. The malignancies are multiple and become ingrained in microchannels simply because of climate. It's pathology grinding out a script.

Nothing could be more critical for brain survival than agency, the ability to threshold with motivation. Lose it and you lose it all.

The intransience of convincing polarities affects the brain. The clouds overhead. The interfaces of potential change. They place the brain in positions of cross-purpose when one lives without referential backdrops to provide escape. Different constellations of firing and wiring construct threshold cities driven by metabolism; sustained by serotonin and dopamine nudges and surges.

That serotonin levels are oddly irregular in thirty percent of autism patients provides yet another sense of how genetic formation is shuffling the deck. These are Autistics in transition from what they were to what they are becoming. These serotonin anomalies provide a 'description' of the upheaval as the organism shifts its dynamics from larger to smaller subjectivity. To misconstrue one's subjectivity is the dynamic behind mental illness. When the mind turns on itself there is no place to hide. Anything swept under the Jungian carpet is surgically laser- lit, engraved irrevocably into need, an absolute last itch effort to be conscious.

Depression is what befell me in 2003... polarities collapsing like matchsticks into a rubble, not of anguish and pain but of nothingness. Indifference. The obliteration of self, of self being organized around what it was once organized – that is the thrust of depression.

Whitehead says that what we add up to subconsciously has much to do with our subjective domain and the measurement and valuation of process. By default, art gets trapped in presuppositions that are in turn galvanized into program and course structures by bureaucracy. The physical integration of temporality is the challenge of every moment. The creative advance of the world is a step into the intuited. It's pure Gestalt. It is NOW, personified.

"It is as though you were sitting in a little sailing boat in the middle of the Zurichsee, and had no idea how to manage a sailboat. If the current was right and the wind was right, you might get to where you were going sooner or later. Or you might bob around indefinitely and get nowhere. Or a storm could come up and you could be overturned and the whole project could end in disaster. But begin the Process, guided by another who has been through it already and cope with the difficulties and found ways to solve them, and it is all different. You learn to take into

account the structure of the boat itself, how it is made and how it responds to the water and the wind. The boat is comparable to your own personality. You learn about the currents in the lake; these correspond to the realities of life in which you are situated and which are somewhat predicable. You learn about the winds, which are invisible and less predictable, and these correspond to those spiritual forces which seem to give direction to life without ever showing themselves. In learning to sail you do not change the current of the water nor do you have any effect on the wind, but you learn to hoist your sail and turn it this way and that to utilise the greater forces which surround you. By understanding them, you become one with them. And in doing so are able to find your own direction – so long as it is in harmony with, and does not try to oppose, the greater forces in being. You may still have to face dangers – there may be swift currents or wild winds at times, but somehow you do not feel helpless any longer,"

(June Singer, Boundaries of the Soul, the Practice of Jung's Psychology, p. 13).

In the summer of 2015, my wife and I also sailed across Lake Zurich in a tour boat. It was very low slung. My camera was virtually at water level.

How is your boat made? Do you sail the depths or stay close to shore?

"Art is best understood as a distillation of pure experience. It therefore provides an excellent and desirable complement to, and enrichment of, the science of mind. As Vienna 1900 illustrates neither approach alone is sufficient to understand fully the dynamics of human experience....Whereas the mathematical and physical sciences involve a specific logic that is powerful for studying and analyzing 'external nature' the study of human behaviour requires a very different type of knowledge, a knowledge from the inside, which he called our internal 'second nature,'" (Eric Kandel, The Art of Insight p. 501).

Once one frames up the mind in terms of Theory of Mind and respective of the intersubjective scale with the Courtney

Spectrum as lens, much is immediately known. It bears repeating: The psychiatry and inter-subjectivity of Psychopaths, Extreme Males, Autistics and Asperger sufferers share very concrete similarities. Absolutely, they share territory in their mental make-up. Deciding on how people get the minds they get is, for the first time in human history, up for scientific analysis. We must assess the veracity of different minds contrasted one to another. We must navigate accordingly.

Jesus on the cross is totally the opposite of tangible power. He has had his ass kicked. He had a sword wound. He had a crown of thorns that caused bleeding on his head. He had been whipped like an animal. Empowerment comes not from the circumstantial evidence of one's life but from the force behind the force behind the force. To not see this is ineptitude and the military can't see it. Like the Sandy Hook shooter, the male likes to take things apart to see what makes them tick.

Agency is directly linked to the emotions, and the motivation linked to mirroring is always the most transfiguring reality of them all.

This engagement with innerness that creativity brings is as personal as it gets. It's the self giving birth to selfness. By choosing to participate in our hyper-extended culture we deny the self.

For Jung, individualism is not a selfish ego making itself known. It involves self-realization, a coming to terms with the infinite wrappings of identity 8 x 10's around the persona trapping it and strangulating it.

MARCH 2017

March 8th, 2017 - International Women's Day. Let's look at stories breaking in the last couple days.

The Marines, 30 000 of them, I believe, have been banking thousands of photos of nude female marines. Also, on this secret drop-box file, are racist comments. What this typifies is not 'boys will be boys. Rather, it typifies boys will be stupid. The Military Mind, as I've stressed in this book, but more so in my previous book, is a jerk-off, unfeeling, monkey-mind. The hatred against women is pure twisted psyche stuff.

The Cubs baseball team disagrees with the MLB hazing policy. They want to dress players up as women for bonding purposes. Hazing is as good as it gets when modern white men try to claim their inner primitive. It is so beset with juvenile psychiatric character disorder, one can't help picture how this figures into the mental make-up of those onside with hazing.

Stories can infiltrate us. As I write today, March 23, 2017, a little blurb tells of the white woman who pretended she was Black and has fallen on hard times. She did great work for the Black brand if you will. Shame on the Black people who brought her down. You are saying what white racists say, there's something to this skin colour charade. She represented ideation of a certain scope and scale that was doing well. In other words, what undermined her efforts was simply the colour of her skin and the white parents who exposed her as White. So what they are saying is: skin colour is something to be prejudiced about, end of story. Too bad.

SPORTS

I played sports. My picture was on the front page of the local paper as captain of the championship Mustangs football team. I was on a championship baseball team. I played hockey until age 15. I boxed at age 28. I made it to the tennis final at Royal City Tennis Club in Guelph ten or so years ago. I sailed, wind-surfed, skied and paraglided   in the Bahamas and Acapulco. I've been up in a hot air balloon several times and in a glider plane three times. I've owned and driven street motorcycles and dirt bikes. I played Senior B lacrosse when I was 16 because our town (now is very different) had no juvenile or junior team. I once scored 7 of our team's 8 goals, in a house league lacrosse championship game. I was on the school volleyball team and gymnastics team. At CWOSSA the district championship I placed 3rd on the pommel horse and 8th on the high bar. I've done judo, squash, and racquet ball. I finished 2nd in shot-putt and discus at a couple major track events, one in Brampton where my bad discus throw almost picked off someone in the crowd. Thank God it didn't. I live close to where I grew up so much of what I say is verifiable in microfilm at the local papers.

I'm not a great swimmer but that never kept me from drowning...Ha ha.

Drowning was a distinct possibility when the wind took my sail board out on Lake Couchiching but didn't want to bring me home. While sailing in a storm on Orangeville reservoir I upended my little Snark sailboat. I swam underneath to free the mast so I could turn it over not realizing my metal mast would sink.

I know the exhilaration that comes with broken field running, when on an end-around you straight arm the corner tackle and find yourself some elbow room, in open field, where you can make things happen. I know the exhilaration of speeding my Yamaha Midnight Special through the Forks of the Credit with its S-bend, hairpin turn. I've had two or three car accidents induced by speed. I like to put the pedal to the metal.

The problem with males is how wrapped up in their ideation they are.

HARD ROW TO HOE

Some women are quickly becoming more and more like men. Many other women have simply subsumed the role they have to play. Just yesterday, a female teacher pled guilty to sexual exploitation and making child pornography. Women, to cut it, often outdistance men in their vileness. A couple of Donald Trump's blonde surrogates are, to my mind, pure evil. There is very little to choose between male and female mentality these days. Though studies show that teenage girls light up their corpus callosum in the teenage years unlike their male counterparts, the outcome is similar...both sexes are shaped by the intrinsic valuing of socially contrived goals.

On Women's Day they talk about how many more women are in corporate executive roles and, indeed, how many more women consider running for president. As long as the measurement of human success is typified by this sort of thinking, the more the human being's formula for success is gravely skewered. Many of the administrators in schools when I was teaching were male.

Some of the despicable were, however, female. They don't mind going in up to the elbows to cut a baby in half. Now they line up for just such an opportunity because it's an experience that grows on some.

MRS TRUDEAU II

Our Prime Minister's wife sent out a message for Women's Day, telling women to give a loving nod to male allies in the feminism fight and to teach sons about respecting women. This is precisely what needs to be acknowledged and it's precisely what I'm writing about. To help the women's cause, you have to educate men; that is first and foremost. Society, including great blocks of women, reinforces ignorance, personify ignorance.

Yesterday, a video was shown of a black man in Canada, I believe near Ottawa, who was unquestionably in my mind, murdered by white cops. The murderer, who landed the decisive blows to the back of the man's head when he was already face down, on the pavement, not moving, is charged with manslaughter. Without the video I'm sure nothing would have happened. Indeed, the top cop completely undermined the role of the SIU (civilian police oversight) mocking it, calling it useless, etc. Other countries think Canada has fewer issues. The fact is: POLICE RULE WITH IRON FISTS in Canada. Nobody challenges them. Left to their own devices, the bad apples spoil the bunch.

I'm white. Unquestionably, most of the true baboons are white male. This is bizarre. I would bet a nickel that society and the world would last centuries longer if all white males were exterminated. Even with intelligence like Brian Williams of NBC news fame, any male has to bend to the 'male' agenda and fabricate macho-ness. Whether it's a shirtless Putin or a parachuting Bush Senior, the modus operandi is pure male. These guys are as far from a Socrates, a Soren Kierkegaard or Jesus Christ as you can get.

I have a great idea. It would bring Trump's psychosis to the surface. A million women carrying signs stating, 'Trump is a Loser.' Donald Trump would have grave difficulty with this. Not to mention a woman playing him on Saturday Night Live.

So women are victims of ideation and this belittles them.

Contradistinctive to this are many of the women at the million women march. A sensitive, intelligent woman like Gloria Steinem transcends all the senators, male and female, in American Government save maybe a handful like Elizabeth Warren.

The brain and universe are almost identical. Glia cells and neurons and firing and wiring precisely are like the universe in action. What you keep in orbit in your life establishes self-replicating criteria. Divorce the emotions and motivational aspects and, all too suddenly, the self is a dead man walking.

A crowd flowed over London Bridge, so many, I had not thought death had undone so many... (TS Eliot)

Anticipation differs from one to another. For some, anticipation means savouring the moments leading up to an event to the point you can almost taste things. For others, it's a vaguely conjured notion, an expectation leaning towards anticipation. We violate our primitive psychic structures with constraint. Constraint ties us to a plot line.

A few years ago, a world famous clarinetist was asked why the clarinet. He said that instruments were passed out on the first day of class and he received a clarinet. Each education is a gift. We need to meet it half way. A clarinet doesn't play itself. If one goes through the lesson route initially one sets up a stylization of how it will be approached. The alternative is to explore the instrument's nature first. Freedom to explore the instrument should predate the learning strictures. In the early going, songs came to Bob Dylan almost automatically. Like Mozart's music, it was there and he just had to pluck it out of the air.

I'm reading a Bob Dylan biography. It's odd that the conscience of a country could be vesselled in a man without conscience and feelings. His promiscuity and his nastiness to friends and musicians is inconceivable. The biographer remarks, **"The controversy caused by Bob's spiritual concerts exceeded even the wildest days of his electric tour, Electricity had annoyed folk purists, but religion bothered everybody," (H. Sounes, Down The Highway, The Life of Bob Dylan, p. 331).**

The anti-religious sorts hurled profanities at the stage, making it a real battleground between Christ and Satan. Non-believers hate believers. The very nature of their reality defies the existence of belief. They have a vested interest in standing up what they stand for.

Our template for feelings is a complex, divined reality. The narrative influences stage processes day to day without stop. Constraint becomes optimized for efficiency's sake in our expedient life styles. The organism organizes a metabolic consequence of which the brain is part. The consequence of our actions becomes our administrator, dishing out oxygen to the brain and invoking upon biochemistry to dictate automaticity. There is a point of virtual no return where neurology hardens like concrete. You can't teach an old dog new tricks.

The chaos of something like regret snowballs, taking on space within the Jungian Complex. But as Leonard says, 'There's a crack in everything, that's how the light gets in.' The reason we are on a better track when at our weakest, drowning, is because constraint itself has inhibited existential sense of self. When everything overwhelms us we must have a better way or there is no point going back to the masquerade ball.

"One must have chaos in one, to give birth to a dancing star," (Friedrich Nietzche).

The elaboration of complexity as potentiation is within the realm of necessary perpetuation. The primordial feed loop is self-enhancing. This is a connectedness that goes back to the primordial energy at the onset of humanity. It wells up within us. Unfortunately, society exercises layers of constraint, artificially determining the nature of what is useful and what isn't. This shapes us away from matters already established in the great chain of being as necessary preconditions for our sustained existence. Preconditions support an expansive brain, a self-aware brain, which knows every neuron is part of an infinite flux that is nailed down by imprinting. Imprinting establishes patterns in our attitudes and hence our psychic construct. A mind can exist with frivolity and distraction only so far. Without sufficiently weighted synaptic actions the mind loses its centre.

Man cannot live by bread alone the Bible tells us. With the onslaught of modernity, the go-to reality has been an objective scientific and secular one. We begin to look at ourselves in an objective way and this is fundamental to how we view ourselves in an increasingly dissociated fashion. We separate from our bodies and our minds break up into sub-sections. The constraints become constraints against holism.

ANOTHER BRICK IN THE WALL

Most significant developments in education have something to it. Such was Differential Learning that recognized and catered to learning style motifs. This is however anti-Theory-of-mind. Only by fusing your consciousness through a common growth do you truly embrace learning. In a classroom energy focal points in a fundamentally human fashion and Glen were two tough guys in my English class the year speeches were mandated. I thought these guys wouldn't comply with doing speeches. The weird thing was, their speeches were amazing. There was something having these guys in the spotlight. We could identify.

In education, for brain plasticity's sake, we should pitch to our weakness to intentionally constellate and capacitate the parts of the brain that are the weakest.

Learning style differentiation tries to fit learning to the student rather than fit the student to learning. We need both things of course. Climbing a mountain where the learning is a hard go, is the most bountiful experience. Differential Learning is destroying such initiative. Most important is the telepathic reality of working through another's mind. By identifying with the nervousness of someone else in a bind solving a math problem on the blackboard, you pump up your identification strength. Post-identification, the mind has an opportunity to 'charge' the system so future identification involves more and more mirroring. It is a capacity continuously growing. It is a major learning attribute.

By killing the arts in schools we are killing the ability to inter-subjectively communicate our most central characteristics – exploration and expression.

All learning is now inferential to a base-line of information accomplishment. It's all there is. Either you get it or you don't. Increasingly, wealth buys credits. The pressure on the system to manufacture slick phonies is irresistible. Noam Chomsky has articulated this in many ways.

It all adds up to an education system with its house built on the sand.

The way we go about information delivery coupled with Differential Learning caters to conditions of separateness.

Separateness without end is a breeding ground for alienation and mental illness. If our students succeed, they become soulless cogs in the information machinery. If they fail, their minds become, often times, their own worst enemy.

 Catering to patterning for autistic children is, to me, catering to the condition.

To me, as I articulated in my last book, we need to emphasize mirroring events. Patterning becomes constraint. The psychokinetic need for time-out rooms for students recognizes the physicality of psychology. Not only can your mind be your worst enemy, your body can become your worst enemy.

For the collective consciousness, the pathology of objectivity becomes more succinct as the pathology of indifference. When people get tired of indifference they turn to violence. Organizational constraints establish themselves as methodology and an overly rigorous finiteness. Collectively we have distorted health, justice and education by dismissing so much as intangible. By fracturing holism we discount ourselves and fall prey to circumstance. More and more scientists are chasing the idea of pill to fix everything. Neuroscience is showing us Subjectivity is a revelation.

The Fast and The Furious topped the box office this weekend for the 3rd week in a row. It has grossed over a billion dollars globally. That says a lot about us. We humans never grow up.

The WASP way of doing things, as I see it, is to sweep the ugliness under the rug. Much of the opposition to Teen Suicide Movie; 13 Reasons, is just such a thing. I believe these issues need to be addressed. The fundamental reason for suicide is: Life is not worth living. It's too boring, it's too nerve-wracking.

We have to drag the matter out into the open. The trouble with White people involves this denial. They see barbarians as having a darker skin colour. A brief look at human history portrays the barbarian not as dark skinned but White. I'm white and I myself always assume the primitive was dark skinned. The true savagery has come at the hands of Hitler, Stalin, Mussolini, The Americans.

It's these assumptions that have brought the White Man to the gates of Hell. The White person, too often, is too arrogant to take the moral high ground of truth.

What neuroscience tells us loud and clear is this: there is no science of sanity.

I hold it true that thoughts are things,
They're endowed with bodies and breath
and wings,
And that we send them forth to fill
The world with good results or ill.
That which we call our secret thought
Speeds forth to earth's remotest spot,
Leaving its blessings or its woes
Like tracks behind it as it goes.
We build our future thought by thought,
For good or ill, yet know it not.
Yet, so the universe was wrought.
Thought is another name for fate;
Choose then thy destiny and wait,
For love brings love and hate brings hate.

(Ella Wheeler Wilcox, in Ye are Gods by
Annalee Skarin)

The Lenny Poems

ONLY ONE OF US WAS REAL

Hi there, he said with fortune's swagger

Are you going my way?

You stood on tip toes till I could barely see

Over your head

The cloak and daggers

you see easily

the nightscape through my eyes before I think it

The sounds of traffic swirling round our feet.

Loaded with vision's spectacle the dance of city lights

pulsing in the night sewers where stragglers kick conversation around in circles.

We held hands and promised to touch before we go to sleep

A touch that touches

a thousand kisses deep

somewhere above my head the slippery sunlight falls

The gaze of distinct splatter along well tested celebrity

ironies that made us, us

Made, you and me, you and me.

Yesterday the room echoed loneliness

And I bounced off the walls chasing words into songs

You were gone the whole day long.

I should stop myself

pacing tiled floors scratching heads

man in melodrama speaks

to mirror with forked tongue

lash him to his own words

full steam ahead.

Shooting down ideas of your solitary pride in flames

I gambol up the hill

I didn't know that I could scream murder

Come on back to the war, don't be so certain

This is love and it's a-hurtin'.

Don't fret, I'm writing out your pardon in Sanskrit

I'm dangling myself off the ledge

I get the subliminal interest in more fastidious grips

The tentative treaty not signed

 ancient voices transcribing some hint of something a la carte

 walk with funeral heads bowed across the flood waters

 around the ark

The pocket change

In the ashes burn etches

holes in yesterday the briefing table

debriefed before we hit the tarmac

the legs folded up under like René Magritte

the incriminating finger printers

Along the vessel's inseam

I paced my soliloquy on the lectern just so

the jurors all ears

The moisture and the panic coming on.

infringed upon their little look-sees and lock-sets

begging their faces draped with eyes and ears

The soft belly of the voice transcribing itself outside in snow-blow slow-mo

We wait on each other to surprise in Montreal

the frenzy we ditched in Winter on Mount Royal

Bits of dialogue chopped in edit

like frozen statues where we used to go.

Waltzing through legal papers

And labouring over details of love and love's labour lost

These consequences lined up on your forehead

The reflection in the nurse's window

embed wrinkles of time in e-mails and phone-calls you can't take back

I tell the jurors this deadness in my eyes

Is not a message they want to hear

They back away in fear

I didn't come to fool you

The ladies go moist and the judge has no choice

The clock strikes 12 and the beach is rolled up and over

There was a girl from Nantucket

Who just said fuck it

Put a noose round her head

And in a second she was dead

I read her memoir in a novel she thought she'd write from the other side

Was nothing to be done?

Nothing comes of nothing

This parrot microchip betrays my ankle bracelet

Scratching at your door

I murder to create and what I create my dear jurors is not for my eyes only

Not for this heart only

Not this part I play only

Not this May Day only

We are less than we think we are.

I used to bring your groceries in

Every night I sit at this table with you

But I can't get high with you

I look past your face and through the window where it rains.

This white flag by design I hang from mercy's angels

The wretched beast is tame

I don't know those people in your picture frame

Guilty as sin the question's apparition answers

How can those dreams be screened by wanting Lazarus?

Simply waiting for the flesh and bone

Pituitary and eyebrow. The body come,

 Slanting at me all scissors and hands

Circumstance and meddling

Which way do you run when the ceiling is tumbling down

When you find your voice pinned to the ankle and your ankle bracelet sticks from rubble and the smoke

before it registers

Everywhere and everything

flesh and dream is on the ground

Of someone else's loss I cannot set the cost

But in the middle of some giant surmise

who knows what cost costs

And soldiers coming back from the war shout and push each other over in the street

Then a child's fear becomes frozen at your feet

and like the lady of the harbour you point your eyes toward the garbage and the flowers,

to anyone who listens for only they can hear

the subtlety of rain wash the features off our faces

where the puddles gather by the drain and people lift their feet

These Dead Sea scrolls of the heart reveal no peeking pulse

no heart bone or sign of shadows leaving marks on the ground

nothing

Draining memory of all its parts

The knee bone connected to the thigh bone

Takes some pulling a part.

It's not something you let sneak up on you in the middle of the night

Nor something you're suddenly at

When framed in the morning's window

Inside the half halting-light

 It's something else

Something different than love or hate

Something stretching airtight over time and space

New skin for an old ceremony

Arriving late

~ November 2016

THE HOLY GAME OF POKER

I'm leaving the table

I'm out of the game

Ode to Lenny

Owed to Lenny

Lenny oh Lenny

oh garden of moonlight, oh shining penny

I walked past

the moments racked and advertised

the pain still shrinking in time-forgotten silhouette

the idea drenched in the rain

first we take Manhattan

then we take it

again and again

see that line moving through the subway

see the daybreak falling on the ground

remember the starched-breath mornings

laughing at us

bent over my cigarette

collapsing in each other's arms

everybody knows you'll live forever

give or take a line or two

written in a Starbucks novel

like it's front page news

we split the dime and nickel, me and you

Travelling light like we always do

we look around at faces floating through the game

we pull ourselves together again and again

staring back reflected in the window panes

The torn raincoat and the silent shore

we're just window shopping you and me

looking for the sun on the wrong side of the street

always chasing ghostly steps till they catch up to our feet.

I let the river answer

you've always been my lover

a scar that leaves no scar

that's you and me

the feverish flame dances stupidly

as if to spring to life again.

Commander Cohen chain smoking behind a snarl or grin

I smile when I'm angry

I lie and I cheat

I do whatever it takes to meet you on the street

parachuting into cocktail parties

in the curdling clouds of night

Amidst the smoke and din

telling anyone in Cuba who might be prone to listen

I've come to fight I'm on a mission.

I'm just a finger painted serviette

hanging out the windows of failing light

a sightless journey's origin

in some Gypsy's wanton flight

Stalking stock moments, laying bare

the threads that disappear in the smiles of the night

Two naked breaths tumbling through eternity

Then fumbling for the switch to turn on the light

I claw at you

you claw at me. We remember.

I gave myself as many burials as I could stand, Lenny

Turned the other cheek not knowing where love might land

We were brothers Lenny, you and me walking through

love affairs like gypsy moths

swinging on the chandeliers

waking in the morning's coma

the world half-disappeared.

The lonely wooden cross yeah

I used to live alone before I knew you.

The famous blue rain coat dragging

me through Trafalgar square

when we finally met up

you weren't even there.

You didn't say a word

Like you didn't even care

You were busy rubbing the world against your thigh

I didn't come to fool you.

if you are fire then I am wood

if you are water I am land

I'll examine every inch for you

I'll step into the ring for you

I held up the bank of love for you

in the middle of the night

So you could pay a debt and put love right

But a man never got a woman back

Not ever

A shift of silhouette in a crunch of streetlight

Still puddles into lonely rooms

In shallow darkness bleeding into light

That's all I can say, all I can write

I'm angry and tired all the time

I just can't get it right.

A pained expression seeking lamplight

Falls for justice in a social smile

in a broken frame there is no one to blame

It all dies like poetry that gets lost in the page.

You need not surrender

I'm not taking aim.

So long Marianne

We'll learn to laugh and cry like we learned to live and die

No big mystery here

From the island in a window

I watch the days chug by

Sinking in a window's sun

Forgetting what I used to remember

All the useless things these hands have done

Can't be me

This heart of ice

must be my double

first we take Berlin, then we go to bed

then we turn and run

and forget everything I said and might have left unsaid

Stacked tea leaves in our heads and some woman's perfumed touch

On the other side of the bed

I beg to differ

too often and too much

It passed for love

Probably still does, I guess

For smudging air in the places where I used to play

I'm condemned to breathe the air we used to share

Like it was something we'd always,

always do again.

I'm not so old I don't feel its soft reprieve

No question these balancing acts

this circus of compromise

The plywood violin

this bending of the knees

has cut the heart right out of me

and when I'm in this window watching

drivers make their lane change

This lonely wooden tower doesn't look the same

The things I'd like to change

We drag down the curtain on this heart

To wipe the tears away

I've never seen your appetite quite this occupied

I never thought to think you could be lying

This Ranger's mask no lonely prone endeavour

We lease ourselves

To shallow graves

We drink the blood and swallow

You can't melt me down in the rain

I'm saying grace

I'm taking my place

I'm like those garbage bags that don't decay.

it's light enough to let it go

the devil is in the details

They say the lady in the tower

is finally saying so

I as much, told you so.

I hurt, I hurt

on the altar of my own self contempt

I've walked these footsteps and waited on the door

The lonely flowers stand

where motion stills the heart beat growing cold.

I follow the pain in circles

This way and that

Whichever way it went.

It still makes no sense

and they've called me on that too.

Where is my gypsy wife tonight?

This flake of life

This serpent's tooth

Communion

A hollow jaw of some lost kingdom

An appetite for the taking

 A moon that runs out of light

in the morning

And when she came home I was - -

Well you get the story

sinking beneath the wisdom

I once owned

It may have been the truth but it's not the truth today.

Take me my lord

My golden voice has had its golden day

I'm almost breathing

Almost human

Almost home

~ November 2016

CIRCUMSTANTIAL EVIDENCE

I'm sorry for that ghost you made me be.

I'm a shining example of a man who's been seduced

but I was **there when she was bathing on the roof**

her beauty and the moonlight overthrew me

the excuses lame

the sisters of mercy licking the same old wounds again

the dove - it will be caught again

the openness of mine a bottle of lipstick down the sink

no time to think

a loose behaviour I will throw off

I will go like **a lamb to the slaughter**

why ask for so much? Why not more?

If you want to take me for a ride

I'm your guy nothing more

I'm last year's man

I've read a review or two

You held onto me like I was some kind of crucifix

The future is now, I'm your man.

Let's go

Now is all we get up for in the tower of song

A banjo kicking smoke a guitar following along

Just a line stolen on a train going

somewhere through a place long-since forgotten

where your mouth had a thousand reviews

shifting the spotlight's focus from me to you.

I can hear you Lenny

I can hear you coughing all night long

All I ever learned from love

I learned from Leonard's songs

how to shoot at someone who outdrew me

how to say goodbye without even knowing

how to say goodbye more than once

on a curb under an umbrella

if you are fire

I must be wood.

Only one of us was real and that was me

We forget to pray for the angels

And they just plain forget

Goodbye Lenny

You knew me

You touched us all

Where it hurts

In the spots that keep us alive

~ November 11, 2016

20/20

Dark are the shadows
that proverbiate

stirring dead ashes of beingness into residue of wood grain

no noonday demon tearing carcasses in the daylight screaming
death to God

Not for me

This death here is a profound death, there is no soundtrack and
the laugh track has died a menacing synapse

The skeleton, the organs, are one lump-sum tissue.

I am carried forth by silence but I got here through anger and
fear.

What's it to you?

I complain about before things and after things not a wit

I marched to the drum of everyday

I brushed my teeth

I deviated from myself

I crawled under covers

avoiding the sum totals malingering in faint whispers

of fiery lashes from a dying room's custom-made voices

I am a heap of broken conversations

I am capsized in my own self.

I am a mental health statistic

I am a smart bomb with invincible decrepit logic

I pool my resources and drown in 3 inches of water

I organize myself around things that go poof

I sift through shadows and stack my image against the boathouse

Where I no longer can float an idea of myself

Everything comes down to an atrophied breath.

Not for the life of me can I muster.

In the snapbook

Those pictures of my walking on water are a lie

Those smiles are photo-shopped

The scandal is in the signature nature

Stooped till it couldn't stoop

Broken so it couldn't break

Dead so it couldn't die.   ~ January 2017

SCREEN

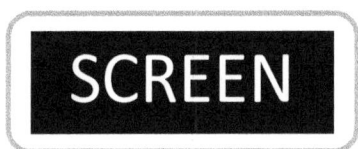

a dramatic play in two acts

a play by David Courtney

SCREEN

The Play creates a character, Lance, who spends much time interacting with his screen, particularly in performing Workshop Growth Material for SET. SET is a brain institute specializing in subjectivity growth leading to life enhancement. A different dynamic comes from the speaker phone where Lance's girlfriend fights to keep him from belonging to the SET cult. The back and forth of this tug of war keeps the 1st act energized.

Characters: Lance
Scarlet
Screen
Iota
Voice (can be pre-recorded or pre-filmed)

ACT ONE

Darkness comes up to light from stage centre to periphery. Man on couch sleeps at edge of light increasingly revealed. **Leonard Cohen's song, Ain't no Cure for Love,** *floods out of the walls. Lance Erikson tosses and turns, gyrating like the song is poison, the memory painful. He pulls the covers over his head. The phone starts ringing.*

The stage, when fully revealed, has a bed centre stage at the back. Above it is a huge screen. Stage right has a desk and lamp and beside the desk is an easel with a canvas. Stage left to the foot of bed is a small fridge and small cupboard.

Then, agitatedly, Lance gets off couch as light levels dim simultaneously as a smaller table light is accentuated on desk.

He grabs journal and scribbles some words down. He looks into the air. The answering machine clicks on. Lance listens to his girlfriend, Scarlet.

SCARLET

Have a great day buddy boy. Remember this weekend we go out for your birthday. Bye. Love ya.

LANCE

(Lance turns back to his journal. Writes some more down. Song stops. He stumbles over to the small fridge. Lance takes glass and fills it. He sets it down. He gets down hands on and knees. He does the Yoga cat stretch. Perking up he stands vertical and stretches then comes stage centre).

(Lance addresses the audience) I must confess if I am to be free I must unburden myself. Anyone who knows anything knows that. As long as I carry the burden it will bring me to my knees, as sure as I am standing here in front of you. So I'm auditing my reality.

Have you ever gone to rehab? You like me perhaps ran into a brick wall you didn't see coming. This is the program I picked to put myself back together.

I did the research. The overall program is called **going solo** utilizing and enhancing self-initiatives in the realm of self-sufficiency. By synthesizing firing and wiring brain patterns the process embodies SET.

SET is the company name. It stands for SUBJECTIVITY ENHANCEMENT TEACHINGS. By altering your mind set you alter the self. WHY? *(He paces back a forth a few steps)*.

Well let's be truthful for once. I, Lance Erikson, have anxiety issues. Besides anxiety issues... I have relationship issues—a grab bag assortment of issues. Everything is so repressed I'm completely passively and violently aggressive in each and every moment.

I'm here to regroup with help from these subjectivity enhancement seminars.

The brochure, much funkier than the Scientology brochure, tells me SET will increase creative flexibility and enhance intersubjective and interpersonal capacity. With SET's help I will develop super-powers or at least an ability to transcend the terrain of my personalized fucked-up-especially-for-me life, littered as it is, with contagious radioactive mistakes. Not to mention hopelessness.

That's me in the corner losing my religion.

My girlfriend believes Enhanced Subjectivity is a scam. She thinks they are preying on my emotional distraughtness. It is true. My emotional distraughtness has pushed me to this point on my event horizon, this point of go big or go home.

SET *(he pauses momentarily for emphasis)* Subjective enhancement has a program, it says, that will let me see though the likes of my girlfriend.

SCREEN, *a voice speaks out from screen*

Lance Erikson... are you there Lance?

LANCE *turns to screen, addresses the audience*

Excuse me.

(On the screen, three Rorschach images morph in and out of each other).

SCREEN

The instructions ... Create a 25 word minimum response in one minute.

(Lance reads his words while image replays morphing Rorschach. A woman under a tree onscreen reads three lines of TS Eliot poetry about the still point of the turning world. Again a 25 word response called response in kind—meaning poetry.

Afterwards, Lance turns from screen to audience).

LANCE

There is no rhyme or reason to SET. It can appear anytime. They – at SET - want their process to refute prescriptiveness. *(He walks 5 paces, visibly mulling this over).*

(Lance walks back 5 paces to where he had been. His tone of voice is reverent but also matter-of-fact). My girlfriend is European. She's different than me. She's cool, calm, deliberative. Subjectivity control has however labelled her as a questionable mate, at best, for yours truly. By the authority of

their investigative intent scrutinizing my habits they have discerned a way forward towards mental health. The way forward may not include my girlfriend. My girlfriend is Scarlet. She's a white rabbit down the rabbit hole sort of girl. Full of magic. At any rate subjectivity central has a different idea. These magical interludes of her are the very aspects of her they find the most disturbing. They think I put her on a pedestal.

The way is the way. That is SET's motto. You only get out what you put in. When you are on the way... *(phone rings)* ... The way down indeed *(he mutters, pushing the button for speaker phone).*

SCARLET, *her voice on speaker phone*

You know, Lance, this is serious territory. You can't think for yourself. SET indeed! This is a set-up Lance. They'll give you the icing on the cake and make you their puppet.

LANCE

You know I appreciate your concern. I'm concerned. That's why I'm here. I don't want this to blow up in my face. You know where I was at, I can't take it. I gotta go - I got to self-activate. *(He hangs up)*

(With the remote control he starts up the screen. Screen is high contrast black and white —trees. Phone rings. He ignores it).

SCARLET, *her voice is heard leaving message on answering machine*

Take care. I'm sorry. *(Her voice pauses briefly and you can hear her sigh impatiently).* I didn't mean to upset you.

LANCE, *freezes image on the screen and calls her back*

I'm sorry too. I'm still on edge. Of course I'm taking it too seriously. That's the point.

I know they might suck me into their reality like you might suck me into your reality, your kind of make believe. I don't know who I am. I'm just a collection of behaviours. In one door and out the next without an inkling of where I 'm going.

SCARLET, *her voice on the phone is heard by audience*

I'm on your side. You keep forgetting that. I'm the one who has got your back. I love you. I have to go to work.

LANCE *comes to stage apron.*

(Lance sits down squat legged, rubbing his head, stretching his neck. The light collapses around him leaving him lit but little else).

She doesn't get it. I'm not supposed to be un-enhancing my mind. I'm supposed to be enhancing it and here I am sounding like a broken record. *(He gets up goes to journal. After a moment he throws pen down and charges stage centre front where he talks to audience).*

305

Now I'm all over the place. Sorry! I don't want to take it out on you. You are innocent bystanders and I've got a history with innocent bystanders. Believe me. Look the other way and the train wreck might be your own. When you go home----- *(Screen flashes on, startles him. JMS 078 appears on screen).*

SCREEN

.JMS 078 ... are you with us?

(Lance has been told he will be randomized and lose his name if his experiential continuity is breached. The screen reminds him of this. His Interim number is JMS 078).

If you aren't with us you are against us. We are trying to help you. A servant cannot serve two masters. Either you want to enhance your subjectivity or not. We will pass into sections 34 A and 79 C. Please pay attention. We cannot subject ourselves to ... *(Phone rings. It's Scarlet calling. The voice on the screen trails off, like an abstraction. On the screen there is a sailing boat sailing across the water. Different camera angles make it kinesthetic. Screen fades 3 times and each time the spotlight finds the back of Lance's head. The metaphor is obvious. The struggle is between him and the screen. Again the phone rings).*

SCARLET, *voice on phone*

I know you are there. I can sense in my intuition that you need help. You need an outstretched hand. You know I love you. You know I am the outstretched hand you need to reach for. Lance I love you. Call me?

LANCE, *walks over and picks up the phone.*
He freezes in thought then hangs up.

(confronts audience) Friends -Romans - Countrymen -   I have
but 5 minutes to get my head right.

SCREEN

JMS 078. *(A woman's face fills the screen instructing Lance).*
Please place blindfold on.

Stabilize your feet and Imagine you are standing atop the CN
Tower on a vertical flagpole. There is only room for your feet.
Raise your arms; hands to shoulder level.

There is a breeze and it is nighttime. The city is a flux of light and
darkness. You aren't looking down. You don't dare take your
eyes off level for the fear of losing your balance. The slightest
movement could be your last.

(At this moment there is loud thunder and intermittently,
barking dogs. The screen shows lightning. Even under the
blindfold his eyes react, but Lance doesn't fall off the tower.
Everything goes quiet. There are bird sounds. Lance stands tall).

Now we do the 'pick-up-your-tent-and-walk' brain modality.
Your switching gears articulates mental agility from CN Tower to
painting to poetry. You know this, but it bears mention to
solidify the modality of interface resolution and resolution for
change. *(The voice is official, as if computerized with human*
qualities, or humanized with computer qualities).

Move your easel stage centre. While standing in front of your easel dab black paint on the canvas. *(Lance removes blindfold, follows directions as if in trance. The canvas will appear on the screen replacing woman's face)*. Now put dots of colour on the mountains of darkness. Take white paint and smear on a face the size of your own face. Surrounding your head will be the lighted darkness.

(Spontaneous overlays of colour. Again and again, like someone possessed, Lance adds and dabs colour. The face disappears in streaks and dabs).

Again we caution - this is a mental agility test ... a change-the-waveband test.

Please respond to poetry in kind. *(Lance sets the brush down. Lance turns to his journal and as he writes, the screen prints the words like a typewriter. Big so the audience can see).*

(Screen speaks lines of poetry) Blistered feet attach hours of grit and around the autobahn you measure the day with cans in your sack.

Every day I peel the layers off empty moments.

LANCE, *responding with poetry*

I feel content to be. To be, I say, and the spirit rises in me to embrace tomorrow. *(Screen goes dark except for red circle).*

SCREEN

JMS 078 this is: this was. You know this one too. This is the biography segment of your life. Last time we showed you pictures of your grade school and high school. We enjoyed your inner child diary.

When we saw you printing with your left hand, we have determined where your right hand was in grade 1. *(Baby printing appears on screen. Awkward letters. Irregular shape).* Hence we accessed your learning-how–to- print brain; the naïve child brain. We have amplified this resonance. We'll work with it soon. This part of the brain is very malleable, very useable. It will be part of our quantum leap down the road.

We have been inspired by your efforts. You have been recommended for elite advancement in our organization. Welcome aboard. You are enlightened. You understand enlightenment. You want more enlightenment. JMS 078 we welcome you into the higher echelons of consciousness.

Henceforward you will be Major Lance. You may even become an Order of Canada recipient.

We will do great things together.

NOW.

We are about to show you sequences of you and Scarlet...snapshots of experience. We want you to see how she subsumes and consumes you. You, JMS 078, are set up by your ego, and its sense of social dynamic, to like Scarlet. Your mind has created a need for Scarlet. *(As the narrative continues there is video of Lance and Scarlet holding hands by a waterfall, spinning on a teeter totter merry go round, eating ice cream and driving in the sports car Scarlet owns).*

As you can see, JMS 078, the symbolic representation of the self creates inner acceptance discontinuous with your actual feelings about Scarlet. Images continue. Scarlet is an X variable. She portrays what you think you want.

We believe Scarlet is the albatross around your neck.

Lie down on the floor and close your eyes. *(The screen goes into psychedelic staccato as the hypnotic voice guides JMS 078 past Scarlet. Phone rings).*

SCARLET, *voice on phone*

Lance you have to call me. Your mother has been trying to get you. She's sick— *(before she finishes the line seems cut off. Sound of beep beep...).*

SCREEN, *voice continues as if uninterrupted*

Poetry.

We are now entering your 11th experiment with Free Association. Your time lapse is exquisite and your mind agile. To this point there has been little difficulty.

This is a verbal visual bridging exercise. Write down a description of each slide. *(Lance grabs journal from desk).*

Okay now look this way. *(What follows is interplay between the Screen and Lance as they move into poetic discourse).*

The ringlets in her hair are ringlets in my eyes; I scour the countryside but find no such eyes.

LANCE, inspired

Wherefore is my love in my despair? I'm so weak with dying, my mind isn't anywhere; the cradle of my misdemeanour cries open.

SCREEN

The perfume of the autumn trees brings sweet summer to its misty knees; my heart like a willow b.ds

LANCE, dramatically spellbound

it could be cold and desolate, and in your bosom a candle held. I'd be so *bold (Lance repeats the phrase with more volume and more emphasis)* I'd be so bold - to hold on to the clamouring heart and make this brief alliance my only truth.

SCREEN

Daylight filters through the trees. I chase my thoughts till they are free. I see the issue clearly now; the very thing in my furrowed brow that love's embrace does dare to hold as moments such as these unfold.

LANCE, *with increasing fervour*

I don't know. My love is lost! - at what the cost - the frenzied moment turns obscurely to the pounding drum, and I am blinded by the sun until my time has come - and who's to say what has been done under the moon, the sun and stars, in every forgetful leap, to who we are. (*Curtain falls*).

END OF ACT ONE

ACT TWO

The dynamic in the first act is particularly is threefold. Lance wanting to rescue himself from mindlessly continuing life on the terms he currently has in place. Scarlet sees Lance who she loves slipping from her grasp, pried away from her by the Narrative Sequencing part of Lance's subjectivity training. Her phone calls are intrusions undermining the platform for Subjective enhancement. Lance is pulled apart trying to keep it all together.

The second act introduces his composite archetypal self - a new delivery service very recently developed by SET. Using Technology of the future SET takes neutrinos and z-particles to cook a psychological transit of the molecular transport, the sort used in Science Fiction. What comes into being is a creature created solely on the basis of subconscious pronouncement, gathered from Lance's own subconscious. This is a composite drawing of Lance's fears. It pops out of the screen. Screen goes blank. Flood light finds the creature, Iota.

Like in Conrad's Secret Sharer story that Jung references, the naked self is swimming into the self as a symbolic but concrete representation. He comes from a psyche architecture non-genetic based reality. While 'HERE' he is an Earthling subject to Earthling rules.

Iota steps back and away from screen and flood light leaves him. He stays on stage, but now in cover of shadow, it is as if he never appeared.

SCREEN

You have done well. We are with you. We are you. You are us. Because of how well your graft has taken we arrive at this very pronounced stage that only a handful of SET graduates have gone. This means vector delineation on unprecedented scale. With symbol, analogy and metaphor, with parable and allegory and time in a bottle you have ascended the spiral staircase into the next step. You are one of the first fish to walk on land.

Because you set disbelief aside you believed with all your heart. *(The screen persona bows to Lance).* Your petty soul is now something to behold. We'll show you brain scans that picture the innumerable amplification coordinates in your neural map.

Because of suspension of disbelief you are operating at a different calibre of self-reckoning. Through the imagination we have accessed features of a non-Euclidian Pythagorean transmigration. It is a fluid principle difficult to functionalize at the molecular level. We have arrived, my friend. You are incarnating History. *(Phone rings. Lance steps over to phone, hesitates, picks it up).*

SCARLET, *voice on phone is edgy, anxious*

I just got the shivers like something is happening to you.

LANCE

I'm supposed to clear my mind and I got four lousy minutes and counting to click out of this reality and into a more receptivity prone outlook.

SCREEN, *echoes, as if a voice out of nowhere*

I can't exaggerate your importance to our program going forward.

SCARLET, *startled, demanding*

Who was that?

LANCE, *splutters, looks from screen to phone and back*

It's the Screen. I told you I've got to concentrate on what I'm doing.

SCARLET

But they are filling your head full of nonsense. They are training you to be a follower. Conformist! They want you to jump through their hoops and forget who you are. For God's sake Lance, don't go ahead with this *(pleading)*.

LANCE

I have to *(somewhat quietly)*.

SCARLET

You can't.

LANCE, *more assuredly, louder than his previous utterance*

It's not training. They don't say go fetch a stick and I go fetch a stick. This is learning for growth not behaviour training. Training is for animals. I have to go. *(With assurance, Lance hangs up phone)*.

SCREEN, *continues discourse as if uninterrupted*

Furthermore to our discussion on the semblance of oratory and the beginning and end of possibility we feature one reality travelling inside another.

We enter the great hall of thought. The dismissal of prescriptive analogue will be virtue. We furthermore agree to disbelieve in disbelief as a pre-emptory condition of our awareness landscape featuring what it will try on for size. *(Phone rings. Lance pauses screen. Answers phone without hesitation)*.

SCARLET

I'm worried about you.

LANCE

I'm worried about me too; that's why I'm here *(pause.)* Don't you remember what I was going through?

SCARLET, *almost exasperated, dismissingly*

It wasn't that bad. Think about it. Bye.

(Lance hangs up phone. Turns back to screen. Holds up remote to release screen from frozen image).

SCREEN

The belief circuitry in our neurology has been eclipsed many times over by the energies of subsequent behaviour patterns. We find ourselves here for the very reason we allowed for a unique resonance in our communication portfolio. *(Screen coughs sputters and dies amidst a flurry of super signals. Light discovers Iota eventually).*

LANCE, *as light reveals Iota, Lance stumbles, almost screams*

Who are you?

IOTA, *steps forward, speaks with absolute certainty*

Who am I? You (*with emphasis*) - messing around with universal energies in composite form and you don't know who I am? I'm your cosmic twin. I'm your doppelganger. In a sense you created me but in another sense I've allowed you to borrow me. I've come from the other side. I've come to bury Caesar not to praise. This is as it is and exactly how it isn't. Energies dance circles around words.

Words are a drop in the bucket.

LANCE, *with disbelief*

This is a bit much. Did SET do this?

IOTA

Of course. SET set it up. So what? What's it to you? You have hitherto subscribed to the Learnings. It is not a bad thing to bend your brain a bit. Nobody's going to bite your leg off.

LANCE

But why? What's the purpose?

IOTA

Indeed. What is the purpose? Now you are starting to get it. Get it? Get set, go. *(Iota chuckles without sound).*

LANCE

You are quite the joker. It sounds like your reality is much different.

IOTA

T'is true, my friend. T'is true.

LANCE

How so? You drive to work in a rocket ship?

IOTA

The bottom line is we see symbols as communication modalities. We see metaphor and analogy as a way out of script zone. We see representational communication as a way of getting on - of dealing with reality.

LANCE

What's that mean?

IOTA

Earth is bundled up in a lot of negative energy. From outer space too we who can see energy as representational can see Earth has fallen on sour times. Nobody comes to Earth any more. It's too dangerous.

LANCE

Dangerous?

IOTA

Very much so. One has to physically prune the representation mind to make it fit Earthling mental atmosphere. Even an Earthling baby prunes away millions of neurons because they can't be used on Earth. The Climate is non-supportive.

LANCE, *contemplates this information, before asking*

Why are you here?

IOTA

You are a graduate. You have intuited this moment.

We want you to find your subjective centre the solar plexus and the heart of the energy endeavour that composes you. As you know this is a highly complex initiative. It makes Rocket Science seem like tiddly winks by comparison.

This is de-contagious and elemental. It will help you live on Earth. It will give you new catalogues of representational thinking. You will be able to manipulate yourself to points of re-surgence.

LANCE, *sits down and massages his head.*

(Minute of pause) And you just popped out of the screen. *(Statement that is not quite a question, expressing disbelief).*

IOTA

Pretty much. Like Jack coming down the beanstalk *(chuckles to himself without sound).*

LANCE

I see you are equipped with the culture dictionary. That - in itself - I find amazing - that you know more about us than we know about ourselves. *(A noise causes both Lance and Iota to look toward the screen. There is sound but no image. The sound surrounds the stage and audience).*

VOICE, *seriously, with weight*

This is a warning of potential Internet collapse. If possible there will be more information coming. *(The message is repeated with the same weight more urgency or less, with more or less speed).* This is a warning of potential Internet collapse. If possible there will be more information coming.

LANCE, *looks away from screen, shaking head, dismissive*

I don't believe it. That's the most ridiculous thing I've heard. *(While Lance is dismissive, and turning away from the screen, the focus is drawn toward Iota who is looking up at the screen with increasing despair. It is his doorway home. A doorway that may have closed. He shrivels down to the floor slowly, like a plant growing in reverse. He curls up in a fetal position on the floor as Lance speaks and softly moans, increasing in intensity, volume and tension).*

LANCE, *staring, watching, unsure*

What's wrong?

IOTA, *lets out exasperated moan/sigh*

Everything is wrong. I can't go home.

LANCE, *uncomprehending*

Duh?

IOTA, *anger rising*

You don't get it. You Earthlings are entangled in prejudice and stupidity. You are like children compared to where I come from. Me being stuck here is un-fucking-fathomable. Imagine you did an experiment that morphed you into an ant in an ant colony. And something went wrong and you couldn't get back to human form. An every day you would live in fear of being crushed.

(Lance is speechless. He opens his mouth to speak, closes it. Steps forward, steps back. Opens it, closes it. Steps forward, steps back. The screen flickers but doesn't come to life).

320

(Iota's anger is replaced by absoluteness). You poor bastards on Earth have suicide structures in the subconscious. Death by History. You are creating a political military reality that has Doomsday written all over it. Why you humans have a death wish is hardly befuddling for we extraterrestrials. You have a fear of failure. You act out failure.

(There is a swell of noise from somewhere in the theatre. It is a rising swell from left to right or right to left, front to back or back to front. Iota stops for a moment, then continues but with increasing agitation. His words are clipped and drawn out at the same time). See the Philistines are on the move. If the Internet is done, truck lines assuring food delivery will never arrive. Airplanes will be crashing. Everything from banking to hospitals to crossing the street - - *(throws up arms)* everything relies on the Internet. You Earthlings put all your eggs in one basket. A virtual basket not a real basket.

Ethereal realms of different degrees of existential gravity we know about.

You guys have to figure this out with comparatively small brains. Your collective-mind is tied up in knots. We can plug into infinitely more dimensionality. But I don't have time to dilly-dally. I have to screen up ways to fix this situation. Or I am doomed.

(Sounds are more and less intrusive throughout the rest of the play.. Much of what happens sound-wise plays off the tension. It's important this works out in terms of stage business and

blocking. Much of this will be worked out when I bring the play to rehearsal.

This is a rough sketch. Before it is performed, what is now merely skeletal will take on more body, more meaning because of the-yet-to-be-incorporated.

Iota explains a little bit about the connection to SET how intersubjective reality is out there and inside us. Scarlet will have lots of questions. We'll get to identify with the three characters through their conversation).

(On Iota's last words, " I am doomed," the theatre has been plunged into darkness. In the darkness we hear the sound of someone knocking on a door. The lights come up on the stage and Scarlet walks through the door onto the set).

SCARLET, striding into the room

Lance, you won't believe what's going on out ther – (she stops mid-word when she sees Iota). Oh, face-to-face training now? *(She pauses and steps back).* That's getting too close for comfort, Lance. *(She looks at Iota and points her finger accusingly at him)* Who are you? I've got the shivers again. *(She looks at Lance, and her body ripples with shivers.*

Lance walks over to Scarlet and takes her hand. The audience sees, but doesn't hear, Lance explain the arrival of Iota, and who he is. During this minute of mimed explanation, Lance gestures towards Iota and the screen. Iota, in turn, gives Scarlet a shy wave, as well as gestures towards Lance and the screen. At the end of this mimed monologue, Scarlet gives another shiver that seems to shake her into the mind space of acceptance. She lets out a loud whoosh of air, as if she has been holding her breath and exclaims) Oh man!

IOTA

Well? ....

SCARLET

(To the audience) Of course I was getting worried. Lance had stopped smoking a couple months ago. He stopped drinking alcohol a month ago. He didn't want to have sex for a month. I thought I was losing him to a cult. Now I see that he was being very dedicated to evolving with subjectivity enhancement. *(She turns and speaks to Iota and Lance)* Okay, okay I can dig it. The empirical fact rules. But how did you get here? You look real. *(She reaches out to poke him in the arm and shoulder).*

IOTA

I'm definitely real, and I'm definitely worried that I might die with you *(he stresses each phrase)*, Earthlings, on your planet, far away from my home. This is no joke.

SCARLET

You have feelings. You have loved ones.

IOTA

Of course. In a sense, we have more loved ones because we have more love. Because we have psychologized ourselves differently from earthlings, our daily agenda is different. We attach different values. Earthlings eat their own tails because love is always conditional on falsely held views. We don't tie the knot like an Earthling couple. For us, love gives us a sense of meaning and security and of ongoing playfulness. That's the major difference. On our planet, love trumps hate. From what we have gathered from planet Earth, you have it all ass-backwards.

SCARLET

Technologically, you must be much more advanced than we Earthlings.

IOTA

Not really. We don't trust technological advancement. We weigh technological advancement against the human cost.

LANCE

But you got here. We can't do that. We can't just beam ourselves up to where you come from. *(His voice gets a little plaintive).*

IOTA

You were on the verge of doing it yourself. SET had set you up, or it, by this transmigration of purposefulness within your own psychic energy. You were heading to Iota. To you, it would just be a place in your head. But that space would grow.

SCARLET, *she looks over to Lance, shrugs her shoulders.*
Lance shakes his head.

I don't think you are computing. I'm lost. We're incapable of understanding what you are talking about.

IOTA

On Earth, your premiere scientist, Albert Einstein, whose name is known throughout the galaxy, called it Spooky Action at a Distance.

SCARLET

Of course! Two entrained molecules can be separated by 2 kilometers or, for that matter, the width of the Universe. If one is interfered with the other reacts instantaneously. Change the spin of one and at the other side of the Universe the entrained molecule reacts. It is Spooky. How can an exchange of Energy happen faster than the speed of light?

LANCE

Don't get her going. She's a graduate student in Physics at the University of Waterloo. She's lectured at the Perimeter Institute. We'll be here for hours.

(There's a loud crash).

IOTA

We don't have hours. Your Einstein said, ultimately there is only the field. He was right. There are unusual properties inherent in the field. But anything in the field is simply in the field. The field is somehow different than time-space continuum. It's just the way it is. Teleporting my beingness here though hmms and haws that involves calibrations not immediately obvious, but as case in point, it fulfills an essential entrainment.

SCARLET

Essential entrainment. Wow. That means essence lined up to essence. That explains a lot but it doesn't happen out of chaos. You navigated here specifically to represent, or so Lance says, his projectiles launched by his subconscious.

IOTA

Exactly. The consciousness of the Universe births the prospect. Consciousness is a field closer to essence than chronology. After integration by way of discussion, Lance would optimize his subjectivity and his teleportation reality. It is like prayer on Earth. We would beam him up, (looking over to Lance) as you said, in a feeling of likeness.

SCARLET

Really? Like prayer? Prayer has its own frequency then.

IOTA

Exactly; like laying on of hands. Energy reaches its kindling point within a psychic field of overlapping personalities bent on one elemental quickening.

SCARLET

Wow, that blows my mind! *(She shakes her head).* We were measuring brain wave cohesion just last week, and encountered unusual spikes we traced back to what we called mutuality alignment. We were on to you. *(She stares at Iota in amazement, her mouth slightly open in disbelief).*

IOTA

For example, the three of us could cross reference and amplify our conductive state. *(Iota takes Scarlet's right hand and Lance's left hand)* by projecting our inner induction states.
(Lance and Scarlet then reach across Iota to hold hands, forming a small circle. Their eyes are closed; their heads slightly bowed. There is silence while they meditate).
(Iota opens his eyes, raises his head and speaks) There - feel that?!

LANCE and SCARLET *speak and move in tandem,*
open their eyes, look at Iota, then hold each other's gaze in amazement

Wo-o-w! *(They say this in a drawn-out way).*

LANCE

That means the three of us could teleport together. That's powerful. Electrical.

IOTA

You bet. I could take you back to Iota Land and I could introduce you to our way of life.

SCARLET

That is so exciting. Think of the possibilities to play out science. *(She pauses, locks eyes with Lance, and then turns to Iota with a slight bounce)*. So, what's a day in Iota land like?

LANCE

Yeah, tell us about your home.

IOTA

It's not different in many ways, but the overall character is different. You Earthlings got afraid of your own minds and pruned away so many capacities. How do you Earthlings put it? - you became afraid of your own shadow. There was always a boogey man under the bed. *(He bends down to wave his hand under the edge of the couch)*.

SCARLET

Like brain plasticity. We moulded our destiny. We came up short.

LANCE

Fear. We were afraid of how civilized we could become. War we understand. Peace we can't get our heads around.

IOTA

There is nothing to fear but fear itself.

LANCE

Heh, that's not Iotan talk, that's Earthling talk.

IOTA

Put that guy on Jeopardy. You're right; it comes with my culture dictionary software.

SCARLET

What's that? It gives you the dope on Einstein and Mickey Mantle and Jackie Kennedy and Princess Di?

IOTA

Oui. And Champs Élysées and poker and Jeopardy and Downtown Abbey. It's a pretty instantaneous download into our functioning memory.

SCARLET

Can we go to your planet the way you came to Earth?

IOTA

Now you're talking! That's exactly it. That's what I said before.

SCARLET

I thought we were talking metaphorically. A space in Lance's head. There are lots of spaces in Lance's head. *(She smiles at Lance and strokes his cheek).* You mean us? - Our flesh and blood selves? We can transport?

LANCE

Okay, okay. *(He walks around in a circle, thinking. There is an echo of voices that circles from left speaker to back speaker to right speaker, encircling the audience like Lance's thoughts).* Would we get a culture dictionary?

IOTA

Of course! We'd make you feel right at home. We download at the speed of your plasticity.

(There's an explosion followed by darkness. The big screen pops on as Lance switches on the light.
A male in uniform comes on screen. Screen blips out).

VOICE, *speaks out from screen*

This is your local emergency task force. *(Audio also collapses).*

LANCE

All hell is breaking loose out there.

SCARLET, *excited, almost begging*

Please tell us more about what Iotan is like.

LANCE, *looks at Scarlet*

Are you crazy?

SCARLET

No, seriously, please.

IOTA

Well, our culture dictionary is much larger. The download will give you a headache for a while.
We have more art than Earthlings. Like your Shakespeare, we have a famous playwright.

LANCE

What do you call him?

IOTA

We call him Courtney.

LANCE

Is that a first name or last name?

IOTA

We only have one name in Iota Land.

SCARLET

That must be confusing.

IOTA

The point of having one name is simple. Here the family is sometimes more important, sometimes less. There is no tradition of 'cupping' as we call it placing familiar dictates on the young. It's a fine line.

Family structures genetic ceilings into breeding. That's why the Egyptian Royals died out. Their strains became uni-molecular. In short, we underestimated the need for chaos when it comes to genetics. Like yourselves, we designed strains emphasizing character traits we acknowledged as good ones. Unfortunately, we got too strained. It was like inbreeding. We were contained in pre-emptive ideas of ourselves created in the minds of our forefathers. So we shook it.

(At the end of Iota's dialogue, light flashes on the screen like a firecracker or grenade).

SCARLET

Let me understand this … So, you took red flowers and white flowers and came up with pink flowers. After years of straining you hit flat spots in the cross-breeding?

IOTA

Very much so.

SCARLET

Like everyone started coming out bald and you couldn't find leverage outside the strains.

IOTA

Exactly. You're a whiz kid.

LANCE

Don't tell her that.

SCARLET, *ignoring Lance's comment*

Why is your name similar to your planet's name?

IOTA

When travelling abroad, exploring extra-terrestrial frontier, we represent Iotan. Any one of us would be called Iota. Still I'm an anomaly. Back home my name is also Iota.

LANCE

Iota like Lakota. (*Scarlet and Iota to laugh*). Has any other Earthling gone to Iota land?

IOTA, *nods head*

Vince.

LANCE

Vince? Who is Vince?

IOTA

Vince is the highest climbing Earthling. He is at the top of SET because his inter-subjectivity found a way to pilot itself through the universe.

LANCE

(*Sings*) Rocket man, I'm not the man you think I am at all. I'm the rocket man.

(Speaks) Apparently, I've made it to the higher echelons of SET, so why don't I know him?

IOTA

SET is anti-hierarchy, anti-guru because one has to be one's own guru and plumb the depths of one's own soul. Gurus are like graven images. People fixate on the personality out there. For true searching it must be avoided at all cost. We are all anonymous sources of energy.

LANCE

Is Vince his name on Earth or in Iota Land?

SCARLET

Sounds like it is sexist there too.

IOTA

I wasn't finished. Three women have made it on their own without the help of the SET's teachings.

SCARLET

Are these teachings good or bad? Is SET a Cult?

IOTA

Not at all. SET is Subjectivity Enhancement, nothing more. It doesn't even believe in hierarchy within the organization.

(There is another series of muted gunshots and explosions).

SCARLET or LANCE

So how did the three wise women do it?

IOTA

It's about belief, or more exactly, disbelief. People tend to dismantle their disbelief before they believe. Disbelief gets to be so huge, most Earthlings never get their heads around it. There are innumerable layers of defence mechanisms configured. You lose the way. You never trust enough to truly let your guard down. Your embrace of life has been thwarted by defensive psychology.

(The screen blinks on and then off, and then on again. The 3 characters watch the screen and then turn back to their conversation).

Once you believe, it's just finding the right wave. Parabola carries you through the fabric which is ultimately as intangible as consciousness. In a blink you spin and counter spin. Voilà. It happens within its own volition.

(The screen blinks on. The next scene happens entirely on the screen, as the image appears, while an authoritative voice speaks. It is the same Voice heard earlier. The Voice might now be a uniformed officer seen on screen).

VOICE, *with authority*

(The image of a uniformed officer appears on the screen. There are pauses between sentences). This is your emergency task force...We want people to not panic... Word that the grocery

335

stores will run out of food has sparked widespread looting... We have to remain civilized. We are turning into a bunch of animals.

(There is lightning on the screen and a woman, dressed in white, appears, holding a bunch of red balloons).

(Voice continues, serious and grim, but resolute) This is serious, my friend. It may indeed be the end. We are inviting you to a red balloon party. An 'end of the world' party. Our rationale is simple. If you want to die with human dignity you will join us. Do you want to reduce yourself to clawing somebody's eyes out? - Someone like you, striving for one morsel of food? For us, that concept is repulsive. Bring your fentanyl and ... OxyContin ... anything that can be packaged in lethal doses. There will be doctors on hand for doses for the children. There is no delusion here. This will make the mass suicide at Jonestown look like a Sunday school picnic. The waft of human flesh will stink to high heaven.

(There is a brief pause and then the Voice continues). That's why we are gathering to the South of the city so prevailing winds should carry the odour across the desert. We don't want to do this anymore than you do. We don't want the children to panic. We want this to be a red balloon party. Red is the colour of passion. It is also the colour of the apple that brought us here.

(The screen flickers and dies).

IOTA

That wasn't the internet. That was local cable. This is devastating news for us all. What a time to visit Earth.

LANCE

Either way, we should go that route. Eat the poison apple. Like
Adam and Eve, and the computer guy - the Enigma resolver ... I
forget his name:

SCARLET

Alan Turing. The Turing machine guy. Yeah, he ate a poisoned
apple.

IOTA

I concur: International reality for you Earthlings means missiles
are being launched as we speak. It's a default security
mechanism that precludes a nation being hacked and made
defenceless. On our planet we have a saying (Iota stands taller
and gives his quote like someone giving a speech): "He who
hacks last gets the last laugh. He who hacks last hacks best."
That's precisely why we transcended the bullshit you Earthlings
are so enamoured of. If I die on your planet I'm going to be one
sad guy. I can't believe it.

(He looks up at the screen. The screen pulses).

IOTA

That's the Internet. Come here. (They stare at the screen,
holding hands. Strobe lighting from behind makes them look like
scarecrows against the screen. Scarlet is in the middle. They
raise their arms in prayer meeting fashion. They are trembling.

There is the most massive explosion with rat-ta-ta-tat small
explosions.

Eventually the screen is all flames.
The song, 99 Red Balloons, plays. Another explosion. Darkness.
The screen is lit up and we see
the three characters are now on screen).

LANCE and SCARLET, *looking around them*

Wow! We made it to the other side!

IOTA

This is it. This is the promised land. (*The song has subsided).*

SCARLET

'Bye Earth. We hope it doesn't go as bad as it seems it's going.

(On the screen there is a parade of human feet, then some jerky
snapshots of mothers and children. People march by from a
slight distance. They are carrying red balloons. In a tighter angle,
the mothers move away from the camera, then towards the
camera.

The song comes to the fore again. As the mothers walk toward
the screen with red balloons tied to their strollers, there is a
sequence of slides/photographs of faces of children and adults
that evoke emotion; babies, pets, animals).

When the song's last syllables come along, the words are filled
with meaning like never before.

The words, THE END, appear on the screen, offered in several
scripts and fluidity morphing descriptiveness. The two words will
fill the screen.

After a half minute of silence there are a couple screaming fireworks. We hear an audio of Woody Woodpecker saying, 'That's All Folks'.

THE END